Breaking Free:

A
Comprehensive
Guide to
Overcoming

Opiate Addiction

Elijah L. Cooley

PREFACE

Welcome to a transformative journey of resilience and recovery. This comprehensive guide is a testament to the collective wisdom amassed over time, offering a beacon of hope to those navigating the challenging landscape of opiate addiction. As we embark on this odyssey together, may the insights within these pages inspire strength, understanding, and a profound sense of possibility.

FOREWORD

In the pursuit of overcoming opiate addiction, Elijah guides us through a landscape of historical wisdom, modern therapies, and personalized recovery plans. This book transcends a mere guide; it becomes a companion for those seeking not just freedom from addiction but a holistic transformation. Elijah's compassionate voice and the diverse array of methods presented create a tapestry of recovery, intricately woven with threads of ancient insights and innovative science.

DEDICATION

Dedicated to Heather, the compass of my heart and the unwavering source of inspiration. Your love fuels the purpose behind this work, and it is a testament to the strength found in connection. May this guide bring light to those in need, just as your love illuminates my path.

Welcome to the transformative pages of "Breaking Free: A Comprehensive Guide to Overcoming Opiate Addiction." In the intricate tapestry of human experience, this book emerges as a guiding light for those embarking on a courageous journey towards liberation from the clutches of opiate addiction.

CONTENTS

ACKNOWLEDGMENTS

I extend my deepest gratitude to everyone who has contributed to the realization of this book. To my family, whose unwavering support and encouragement have been the bedrock of my journey, thank you for standing by me through every twist and turn. To my friends and colleagues, your insights and feedback have been invaluable in shaping the ideas presented in these pages. I am also grateful to the countless individuals who shared their stories and experiences with me, shedding light on the complexities of opiate addiction and recovery. Your courage and resilience inspire me every day. Special thanks to the healthcare professionals, researchers, and advocates who tirelessly work to combat addiction and improve the lives of those affected. Your dedication to this cause is truly commendable. Lastly, I want to express my appreciation to the readers who have chosen to embark on this journey with me. It is my sincere hope that this book offers insights, support, and hope to anyone grappling with opiate addiction, as well as to their loved ones. Thank you all for being part of this important conversation.

1 CHAPTER

UNDERSTANDING OPIATE ADDICTION

In the shadows of personal struggles, opiate addiction stands as a formidable adversary, its grip extending beyond the physical to the depths of the mind and soul. This chapter peels back the layer revealing the intricate nature of opiate addiction and laying the groundwork for the transformative journey ahead.

Unraveling the Chains

Opiate addiction is a complex tapestry woven with threads of physical dependence and psychological entanglement. At its core, it involves the brain's adaptation to the presence of opiates, leading to a state where the body craves these substances to maintain a semblance of normalcy. Understanding this intricate dance between biology and behavior is pivotal in confronting the profound grip of addiction.

The Neurobiology of Addiction

We delve into the neurobiology of addiction, exploring how opiates hijack the brain's reward system. Dopamine, the neurotransmitter associated with pleasure and reward, becomes a central player, creating a cycle of dependency that intensifies with each use. This biochemical dance is a critical factor in the compulsion to seek and use opiates, forming the foundation of the addiction's stronghold.

The Psychological Landscape

Beyond the physiological aspects, opiate addiction leaves an indelible mark on the psychological landscape. The allure of escape from pain, both physical and emotional, often sets the stage for the initial encounter with opiates. As reliance grows, the original motivations become intertwined with the relentless pull of addiction, creating a web that can seem insurmountable.

Breaking the Silence

Understanding opiate addiction is not just an intellectual pursuit; it is an emotional reckoning. This chapter amplifies the voices of those who have faced the silent struggles, providing a platform for shared experiences. By breaking the silence surrounding addiction, we diminish the stigma that often shrouds it, fostering an environment of empathy and understanding.

Facing the Impact

The impact of opiate addiction extends far beyond the individual. Families, communities, and societies bear the weight of its consequences. Examining this broader impact underscores the urgency of finding effective solutions. It's a call to action, challenging us to address not only the symptoms but the root causes of addiction.

The Path Forward

As we unravel the intricacies of opiate addiction in this chapter, we lay the groundwork for the chapters that follow. Armed with knowledge, empathy, and a commitment to understanding, readers are poised to confront their own journeys. "The Grip of Addiction" serves as a compass, guiding us through the uncharted territory of recovery and illuminating the path towards breaking free.

Section II:

Exploring the Physiological and Psychological Aspects

Physiological Underpinnings

As we delve deeper into the labyrinth of opiate addiction, it's essential to unravel the physiological underpinnings that characterize this complex relationship between the human body and these powerful substances. Opiates, whether derived naturally from the opium poppy or synthetically produced, exert their influence on the central nervous system with profound implications. The journey begins at the molecular level, where opiates bind to specific receptors in the brain—primarily the mu-opioid receptors. This interaction triggers a cascade of events, inhibiting the release of neurotransmitters that regulate pain perception and mood. The result is a numbing effect, providing both physical and emotional relief. However, this relief comes at a cost—the recalibration of the brain's reward system.

Neuroplasticity and Adaptation

Opiate use induces neuroplastic changes, rewiring the brain to accommodate the constant presence of these substances. Over time, the brain adapts to the altered balance of neurotransmitters, creating a new baseline that necessitates continued opiate consumption to maintain equilibrium. This neuroadaptation forms the crux of physiological dependence, marking the inception of the addiction's stronghold.

Psychological Dimensions

The physiological entanglement of opiates extends its tendrils into the realm of psychology. The initial allure of opiates often lies in their ability to provide a respite from emotional pain or distress. Whether driven by chronic physical pain or underlying mental health issues, individuals find in opiates a temporary escape, a refuge from the tumultuous currents of life.

Cycles of Craving and Compulsion

As opiates become a coping mechanism, a cycle of craving and compulsion takes root. The brain, now accustomed to the artificial surge of pleasure induced by opiates, signals a relentless urge for more. This interplay between physiological dependence and psychological yearning creates a self-sustaining loop that defines addiction.

Breaking the Cycle

Understanding these intertwined physiological and psychological dimensions is the cornerstone of recovery. It unveils the nature of the battle that individuals face, emphasizing the importance of holistic approaches that address both the physical and emotional facets of addiction. In the chapters to come, we explore strategies to disrupt this cycle, empowering individuals to reclaim control over their physiological responses and psychological well-being. In this exploration, we lay bare the intricate dance between body and mind, acknowledging the multifaceted nature of opiate addiction. The journey toward breaking free requires a comprehensive understanding —one that encompasses both the physiological grip and the psychological echoes that reverberate through the corridors of addiction

Section III:

Impact on Individuals and Communities

Individuals in the Shadows

As we navigate the intricate landscape of opiate addiction, it's essential to illuminate the shadows where individuals grapple with the profound impact of this affliction. Opiate addiction is not a solitary struggle confined to the walls of one's existence; its tendrils extend, affecting relationships, aspirations, and the very fabric of daily life.

Physical and Mental Toll

At an individual level, the toll of opiate addiction is evident in the physical and mental realms. Physically, the body undergoes a relentless battle, facing health deterioration, compromised immune function, and an increased vulnerability to various ailments. Mental well-being is equally affected, with anxiety, depression, and cognitive impairments becoming unwelcome companions on this harrowing journey.

Strained Relationships

Within the scope of personal relationships, opiate addiction casts a long shadow. The trust that forms the foundation of connections erodes, replaced by a pervasive sense of uncertainty and betrayal. Loved ones witness the transformation of someone they once knew into a stranger consumed by the relentless demands of addiction.

Economic Burden

The impact extends beyond the emotional and physical, infiltrating the economic fabric of communities. Individuals grappling with addiction often find their professional lives in disarray—employment instability, financial strain, and a diminished capacity to contribute to the workforce. The economic burden is not borne solely by those ensnared by addiction but resonates throughout communities.

Communal Repercussions

Zooming out to the broader scope, communities grapple with the collective repercussions of opiate addiction. Strained healthcare systems, increased crime rates, and the erosion of social cohesion are ripples that extend from the epicenter of addiction. The burden on public services, from law enforcement to healthcare, further underscores the far-reaching consequences of this pervasive issue.

Destigmatizing the Struggle

Understanding the impact on individuals and communities is a call to action. It beckons us to destigmatize the struggle, fostering an environment of empathy and support. By recognizing addiction not as a moral failing but as a complex health issue, communities can pave the way for comprehensive solutions that address both prevention and recovery.

Hope in Collective Action

Yet, even amid the shadows, there is hope. The collective action of individuals, families, and communities can become a powerful force in dismantling the barriers to recovery. By fostering understanding, empathy, and open dialogue, we begin the journey toward healing not only for the individuals facing addiction but for the communities that stand resilient in the face of this shared challenge. In unraveling the impact on individuals and communities, we lay the groundwork for the chapters ahead—exploring strategies, insights, and collective endeavors that lead to a comprehensive understanding of opiate addiction and, ultimately, the path to breaking free.

Section IV

Understanding Broader Implications: Personal and Societal Levels

Interconnected Narratives

Opiate addiction reverberates across the intricate tapestry of personal and societal narratives. Beyond individual struggles and community impacts, it casts a profound shadow on the very fabric of society, demanding our attention and collective effort to unravel its broader implications.

Societal Undercurrents

The narrative extends beyond the individual, intertwining with societal undercurrents. Opiate addiction is not a solitary phenomenon; it is symptomatic of deeper societal issues—economic disparities, inadequate access to healthcare, and a broader cultural context that often stigmatizes mental health struggles. To comprehend the broader implications, we must delve into these interconnected layers.

Economic Disparities

The economic toll of opiate addiction extends beyond personal finance to broader economic disparities. As individuals face employment challenges, communities witness a ripple effect in reduced productivity and strained public services. The economic burden becomes a shared challenge, highlighting the need for systemic solutions that address both the roots and manifestations of addiction.

Healthcare Systems Strain

The strain on healthcare systems is a tangible consequence of opiate addiction's broader implications. Emergency rooms grapple with overdose cases, while addiction treatment facilities strain to meet the growing demand for services. This not only impacts individuals directly affected by addiction but places an undue burden on healthcare infrastructure, necessitating comprehensive reform.

Educational and Legal Ramifications

Schools and legal systems navigate the repercussions of opiate addiction as well. Educational institutions witness the indirect effects— students grappling with familial addiction may face academic challenges, perpetuating cycles of disadvantage. The legal system, burdened by substance-related offenses, struggles to balance punitive measures with rehabilitation.

Cultural Shifts and Stigma

Culturally, the stigma surrounding addiction perpetuates a cycle of silence and shame. Understanding opiate addiction's broader implications requires a cultural shift—one that replaces judgment with empathy, recognizing addiction as a health concern rather than a moral failing. This shift is pivotal in dismantling barriers to treatment and fostering a society where individuals feel empowered to seek help without fear of condemnation.

The Call to Action

As we navigate these broader implications, it becomes evident that overcoming opiate addiction requires a multi-faceted approach. The call to action is not just individual but societal, demanding a collective commitment to systemic change, destigmatization, and accessible resources for prevention and recovery. In understanding the broader implications of opiate addiction on personal and societal levels, we illuminate the intricate threads that weave through the narrative of this complex issue. This comprehension serves as the foundation for the chapters ahead—a journey that seeks not only to understand but to actively address the multifaceted challenges posed by opiate addiction.

2 CHAPTER

HISTORICAL METHODS: WISDOM FROM THE PAST

Ancestral Narratives of Resilience

In delving into historical methods of overcoming opiate addiction, we unearth ancestral narratives steeped in resilience and the human capacity for transformation. The stories of our predecessors echo through time, offering profound insights into strategies that have withstood the test of generations—wisdom forged in the crucible of shared struggle.

Herbal Remedies and Alchemy

Our journey commences with the wisdom of ancient civilizations, where herbal remedies and alchemy were employed to address various ailments, including the challenges of addiction. The rich tapestry of traditional healing practices reveals a holistic approach that integrated physical, mental, and spiritual elements, recognizing the interconnectedness of the human experience.

Rituals of Purification

Many cultures embraced rituals of purification to cleanse the body and spirit from the clutches of addiction. These rituals, often intertwined with spiritual practices, were symbolic journeys of renewal—a collective acknowledgment that overcoming addiction requires a transformative process that extends beyond the physical realm.

Community Support and Accountability

Central to historical methods was the emphasis on community support and accountability. In close-knit societies, individuals facing addiction were not isolated but surrounded by a network of understanding and support. The communal approach recognized the shared responsibility of helping individuals navigate the challenges of recovery.

Mind-Body Practices

Ancient civilizations also revered mind-body practices as vehicles of healing. Techniques such as meditation, breathwork, and yoga were employed not only to cultivate inner peace but also to fortify th against the tumultuous currents of addiction. These practices, rooted in mindfulness and self-awareness, remain relevant guides in the contemporary pursuit of recovery.

Cultural Narratives of Triumph

Beyond specific methods, historical approaches to overcoming addiction were embedded in cultural narratives of triumph over adversity. Myths, legends, and religious stories depicted individuals who faced and conquered the trials of substance dependence, offering archetypal models of strength, perseverance, and redemption.

Integration into Modern Recovery

As we explore these historical methods, the intention is not to romanticize the past but to distill timeless principles that can inform modern recovery. Wisdom from the past becomes a wellspring of inspiration—a reminder that our ancestors, too, grappled with the complexities of addiction and forged paths toward healing. This chapter invites readers to draw from this reservoir of historical insight, integrating age-old wisdom into the contemporary tapestry of recovery.

Examining Time-Tested Tradition: Enduring Practices

As we navigate the historical landscape of overcoming opiate addiction, it is essential to scrutinize traditional methods that have proven their resilience over time. These enduring practices are not relics of the past but living testaments to the human capacity for innovation and adaptation in the face of challenges.

Acupuncture and Traditional Chinese Medicine

One such time-tested tradition emerges from the realms of Traditional Chinese Medicine (TCM). Acupuncture, a cornerstone of TCM, has been employed for centuries to restore balance in the body's energy flow. In the context of addiction, acupuncture aims to alleviate withdrawal symptoms, reduce cravings, and foster overall well-being. This holistic approach recognizes the interconnectedness of physical and mental health.

Ayurveda and Herbal Remedies

The ancient wisdom of Ayurveda, originating from India, provides another layer of insight. Ayurvedic practices leverage herbal remedies, dietary adjustments, and lifestyle modifications to restore equilibrium in the body's doshas—vital energies. This comprehensive approach addresses not only the symptoms of addiction but seeks to rectify imbalances at their root.

Native American Healing Traditions

Native American healing traditions offer profound wisdom in the form of rituals, ceremonies, and herbal remedies. The emphasis on reconnecting with nature and fostering a harmonious relationship with the environment resonates in the context of addiction recovery. These traditions highlight the transformative power of spiritual practices in the healing journey

Greek Philosophy and Self-Reflection

Turning our gaze to ancient Greece, we find philosophical traditions that promoted self-reflection and moderation. Socratic questioning, as an element of philosophical discourse, encouraged individuals to introspect and confront the underlying causes of addiction. This approach, grounded in self-awareness and rational inquiry, remains pertinent in contemporary therapeutic practices.

Healing through Rituals

Rituals, a common thread in various cultures, emerge as potent tools for healing. Whether the ceremonial purification rites of indigenous cultures or the structured rituals of ancient societies, these practices symbolize a deliberate commitment to transformation. The power lies not just in the acts themselves but in the intentionality behind each ritual—a dedication to breaking free from the chains of addiction.

Legacy of Resilience

As we examine these traditional methods, we discern a common thread — the legacy of resilience woven into the fabric of diverse cultures. These practices are not frozen in time; they are dynamic, evolving, and adaptable. The examination of historical methods is not a mere homage to the past; it is a quest to distill enduring principles that can inform the contemporary pursuit of recovery. In the chapters that follow, we explore how these historical treasures can be integrated into modern methodologies, offering a bridge between ancient wisdom and the evolving landscape of addiction recovery.

Section II

Bridging the Past and Present: Incorporating Historical Wisdom

Relevance of Ancient Insights

As we traverse the corridors of history in search of methods to overcome opiate addiction, it becomes evident that the wisdom of the past is not confined to antiquity; it holds relevance in the contemporary landscape of recovery. In this section, we explore the seamless integration of historical insights into modern methodologies—a bridge between ancient wisdom and the evolving needs of today.

Adapting Ancient Healing to Modern

Science The foundational principles of ancient healing traditions, such as Traditional Chinese Medicine (TCM) and Ayurveda, resonate with modern science. The incorporation of acupuncture into contemporary recovery programs is a testament to the adaptability of these ancient practices. Scientific research supports acupuncture's efficacy in reducing withdrawal symptoms and addressing the neurobiological aspects of addiction.

Herbal Remedies in Modern Medicine

Herbal remedies, a staple in historical healing, find a place in modern medicine's evolving approach to recovery. From detox teas to supplements targeting neurotransmitter balance, the integration of herbal wisdom provides a holistic dimension to contemporary treatment plans. This intersection of ancient herbal knowledge with evidence-based practices underscores the value of a comprehensive approach.

Cultural Competency in Treatment

Recognizing the cultural roots of traditional healing practices is integral to incorporating historical wisdom into modern recovery. Tailoring treatment plans to honor diverse cultural perspectives fosters a sense of inclusivity and understanding. This cultural competency acknowledges that the journey to recovery is deeply personal and influenced by one's cultural background.

Mindfulness and Meditation Practices

Mindfulness and meditation, ancient tools for cultivating inner peace, have found a prominent place in modern recovery. Incorporating these practices into therapeutic interventions addresses the psychological aspects of addiction. Mindfulness-based approaches, such as Mindfulness-Based Stress Reduction (MBSR), provide individuals with practical tools to navigate cravings and enhance self-awareness.

Community Support Models

The emphasis on community support, a cornerstone of historical methods, aligns with contemporary models such as 12-Step programs. The power of peer support, accountability, and shared experiences remains a guiding force in modern recovery. Community-based initiatives and support groups draw inspiration from the communal ethos that has withstood the test of time.

Rituals of Reflection and Renewal

Rituals, imbued with symbolic significance, have evolved to meet the needs of modern recovery. Structured activities that encourage self-reflection, commitment ceremonies, and rites of passage mirror the transformative essence of historical rituals. These contemporary adaptations provide individuals with a tangible framework for breaking free from the cycle of addiction.

The Living Tapestry of Recovery

As we weave historical wisdom into the fabric of contemporary recovery, it becomes a living tapestry—a synthesis of ancient insights and modern advancements. This integration is not about recreating the past but recognizing the enduring principles that transcend time. In the chapters ahead, we delve deeper into the practical application of these integrated approaches, offering a roadmap for individuals seeking recovery in a world that bridges the wisdom of yesterday with the possibilities of tomorrow

3 CHAPTER

MODERN THERAPIES

Section I
Cognitive-Behavioral Therapy (CBT)

Navigating the Mind's Terrain

In the expansive realm of modern therapies for overcoming opiate addiction, Cognitive-Behavioral Therapy (CBT) emerges as a guiding beacon— a therapeutic approach that navigates the intricate terrain of thoughts, emotions, and behaviors. Rooted in psychological principles, CBT is a versatile and evidence-based tool that empowers individuals to transform their relationship with addiction.

Understanding the Core Tenets

At the heart of CBT lies the recognition that thoughts, feelings, and behaviors are interconnected. The therapy unfolds through a collaborative exploration between the individual and the therapist, focusing on identifying and challenging negative thought patterns that contribute to addictive behaviors. By understanding the underlying beliefs driving these patterns, individuals gain insights that form the foundation for lasting change.

Breaking the Cycle of Craving and Use

One of CBT's core objectives is breaking the cycle of craving and substance use. Through a process known as functional analysis, individuals dissect the chain of events leading to substance use, identifying triggers, thoughts, and emotional states. Armed with this awareness, they collaboratively develop coping strategies to interrupt this cycle, gradually reclaiming control over their responses to cravings.

Skill-Building for Coping and Resilience

CBT is not merely introspective; it's action-oriented. Individuals learn practical skills for coping with stress, managing emotions, and navigating challenging situations without resorting to substance use. These skills, often referred to as coping mechanisms, become powerful tools in the toolkit of recovery, fostering resilience in the face of life's complexities.

Addressing Co-Occurring Issues

Recognizing the interconnected nature of mental health and addiction, CBT shines as an effective approach for addressing co-occurring issues. Individuals grappling with anxiety, depression, or trauma often find relief in CBT's tailored strategies. By addressing these underlying concerns, CBT contributes to a more comprehensive and holistic recovery journey.

Empowering Personal Responsibility

CBT empowers individuals by fostering a sense of personal responsibility. Through the therapeutic process, individuals learn to recognize their agency in the recovery journey. This sense of empowerment becomes a driving force, fueling motivation and resilience—a departure from a passive role to an active participant in one's own transformation.

Adaptability to Diverse Needs

One of CBT's strengths lies in its adaptability to diverse needs and preferences. Whether delivered individually or in group settings, faceto-face or through digital platforms, CBT molds itself to accommodate varying lifestyles and preferences. This flexibility ensures that the therapeutic benefits of CBT are accessible to a broad spectrum of individuals seeking recovery. The Journey Forward. As we embark on the exploration of modern therapies, CBT stands tall as a cornerstone—a versatile and potent ally in the pursuit of recovery. Its principles, deeply rooted in understanding and transforming thought patterns, empower individuals to rewrite their narratives and forge a path towards sustained healing. In the chapters ahead, we delve into additional modern therapies that complement and enrich the recovery landscape.

Section II
Cognitive-Behavioral Therapy (CBT): Practical Applications and Success Stories

Practical Applications

The strength of CBT lies not only in its theoretical underpinnings but in its practical applications that resonate in the daily lives of those navigating opiate addiction recovery. One of its key applications is the development of coping skills. Through CBT, individuals acquire concrete strategies to manage stress, handle triggers, and navigate situations that might otherwise lead to substance use. Another practical application is the collaborative nature of goal-setting. Individuals, in tandem with their therapists, identify specific, realistic goals tailored to their unique circumstances. This goal-oriented approach provides a roadmap for progress, fostering a sense of achievement and motivation throughout the recovery journey.

Success Stories: A Glimpse into Transformation

Embedded within the fabric of CBT are countless success stories—a testament to the transformative power of this therapeutic approach.

Sarah, once ensnared in the throes of opiate addiction, found solace in CBT's emphasis on understanding and challenging negative thought patterns. By unraveling the cognitive threads that fueled her substance use, she cultivated resilience and now champions a life free from addiction.

Mark's success story showcases the practical skills acquired through CBT. Battling cravings and facing triggers, he applied coping mechanisms learned in therapy to navigate challenges. Mark's journey demonstrates how the tangible tools acquired in CBT empowered him to break free from the cycle of addiction and build a foundation for lasting recovery.

Enhancing Emotional Regulation

CBT excels in enhancing emotional regulation—a critical aspect of overcoming addiction. Emma, whose opiate use was closely tied to emotional struggles, found CBT instrumental in understanding and managing her emotions. Through the therapy's techniques, she developed emotional resilience, diminishing the need for substances as a coping mechanism.

John's success story illustrates the adaptability of CBT to co-occurring issues. Wrestling with anxiety alongside his opiate addiction, John discovered relief through CBT's targeted strategies for addressing mental health concerns. His journey highlights how a comprehensive approach that integrates mental health and addiction treatment can lead to sustainable recovery.

Holistic Impact on Well-Being

The success stories within the realm of CBT echo beyond the cessation of substance use—they encompass a holistic impact on well-being. Rachel, embracing CBT's focus on personal responsibility, not only conquered her opiate addiction but experienced a profound shift in self-perception. This holistic transformation underscores the potential for CBT to catalyze a comprehensive reevaluation of one's life and priorities.

The Continuing Narrative of Recovery

As we delve into the practical applications and success stories of CBT, the chapters ahead will unfold additional modern therapies, each contributing its unique perspective to the narrative of recovery. CBT stands as both a foundational pillar and an inspiring model—a testament to the possibility of not only breaking free from addiction but embarking on a journey of profound personal growth and resilience.

Section III

Medication-Assisted Treatments (MAT)

A Holistic Approach to Recovery

In the dynamic landscape of modern therapies for opiate addiction, Medication-Assisted Treatment (MAT) emerges as a comprehensive strategy, combining pharmacological interventions with therapeutic support. MAT is rooted in the understanding that addiction is a complex, multifaceted condition, and addressing its physiological components is integral to fostering lasting recovery.

Pharmacological Allies in Recovery

At the forefront of MAT are medications specifically designed to alleviate withdrawal symptoms, reduce cravings, and mitigate the physiological effects of opiate dependence. Suboxone, methadone, and naltrexone are among the pharmacological allies that play pivotal roles in supporting individuals through different phases of recovery. These medications are carefully prescribed and monitored, forming a crucial component of a personalized treatment plan.

Reducing Cravings and Withdrawal

MAT's effectiveness lies in its ability to alleviate the intense cravings and withdrawal symptoms that often accompany opiate addiction. By targeting the same receptors in the brain affected by opiates, these medications provide a controlled and regulated alternative, minimizing the disruptive impact of withdrawal and enabling individuals to focus on their recovery journey.

Long-Term Maintenance and Relapse Prevention

MAT extends beyond the initial phases of recovery, offering long-term maintenance options. This is particularly significant for individuals with chronic opiate dependence. Maintenance medications provide stability, reducing the risk of relapse and creating a foundation for individuals to rebuild their lives without the constant threat of withdrawal or intense cravings.

Integration with Therapeutic Support

Crucial to MAT's success is its integration with therapeutic support. Counseling and behavioral therapies, when combined with medication, create a synergistic effect. This combination addresses both the physiological and psychological aspects of addiction, enhancing the overall effectiveness of the treatment. Therapy sessions provide a space for individuals to explore the root causes of their addiction, develop coping strategies, and foster essential life skills.

Personalizing Treatment Plans

MAT is not a one-size-fits-all approach. Treatment plans are meticulously personalized based on an individual's unique needs, medical history, and response to medications. Regular monitoring ensures adjustments can be made as necessary, tailoring the approach to evolving circumstances and ensuring the most effective and supportive treatment journey.

Success Stories: Navigating the Journey

Success stories within MAT are diverse and profound. Sarah's journey exemplifies how MAT, coupled with counseling, empowered her to regain stability and rebuild her life. With reduced cravings and the support of therapy, she transitioned from the shadows of addiction to a life marked by resilience and hope.

Towards Comprehensive Recovery

As we explore MAT's role in modern therapies, it becomes evident that its integration into the recovery landscape offers a multifaceted approach—one that recognizes the intricate interplay between physical and psychological well-being. In the chapters to come, we will delve into additional modern therapies, each contributing its unique perspective to the ongoing narrative of recovery.

Section IV
Pharmacological Interventions in Opiate Addiction Treatment

Navigating the Neurochemical Landscape

In the intricate terrain of opiate addiction treatment, pharmacological interventions form a crucial component, addressing the neurochemical imbalances that underpin dependence. These medications, carefully prescribed and monitored, play distinct roles at various stages of the recovery journey, offering relief from cravings, withdrawal symptoms, and the physiological challenges that accompany opiate addiction.

Methadone: Stabilizing the Journey

Methadone, a long-acting opioid agonist, occupies a central role in pharmacological interventions. By binding to the same receptors as opiates, it mitigates withdrawal symptoms and cravings without inducing the euphoria associated with stronger opioids. Administered in a structured clinical setting, methadone provides stability, allowing individuals to engage in daily activities without the disruptive influence of withdrawal.

Buprenorphine/Naloxone (Suboxone): Balancing Act

Suboxone, a combination of buprenorphine and naloxone, is a partial opioid agonist. Buprenorphine alleviates withdrawal symptoms and cravings, while naloxone acts as a deterrent to misuse. Suboxone's unique profile reduces the risk of dependence while providing a controlled alternative. Its effectiveness is coupled with a lower risk of respiratory depression, making it a safer choice for long-term maintenance.

Naltrexone: Blocking the Effects

Naltrexone takes a different approach by blocking opioid receptors, rendering opiates ineffective. This antagonist disrupts the reinforcing effects of opioids, acting as a deterrent against relapse. Available in oral and extended-release injectable forms, naltrexone is a valuable tool for individuals committed to maintaining abstinence. Its nonaddictive nature and lack of withdrawal symptoms contribute to its appeal in relapse prevention.

Success Stories: Resilience in Recovery

Maggie's success story illustrates the transformative impact of pharmacological interventions. Methadone, carefully administered, provided the stability she needed to rebuild her life. Over time, Maggie transitioned to lower doses, eventually freeing herself from the clutches of dependence. Her journey underscores the role of methadone as a stabilizing force in the recovery narrative.

Comprehensive Treatment Approaches

Pharmacological interventions are most effective when integrated into comprehensive treatment approaches. The combination of medication with counseling, therapy, and support groups creates a holistic framework that addresses both the physical and psychological aspects of addiction. These interventions are not standalone solutions but integral components of a nuanced and individualized treatment plan.

Ongoing Research and Innovation

The landscape of pharmacological interventions in opiate addiction treatment is dynamic, with ongoing research exploring new medications and delivery methods. From extended-release formulations to emerging medications targeting specific neuroreceptors, the field continues to evolve, offering hope for even more tailored and effective approaches to addiction treatment.

A Collaborative Path Forward

As we traverse the realm of pharmacological interventions, the chapters ahead will unveil additional modern therapies, each contributing to the evolving narrative of recovery. The integration of these interventions reflects a collaborative path forward—a synthesis of medical advancements, therapeutic support, and individual resilience that defines the contemporary landscape of opiate addiction treatment.

4 CHAPTER

HOLISTIC HEALING

Section I
Mindfulness and Meditation: Nurturing Inner Resilience

Journey into the Present Moment

In the pursuit of holistic healing for opiate addiction, the realms of mindfulness and meditation emerge as transformative allies. Rooted in ancient contemplative traditions, these practices invite individuals to journey into the present moment, cultivating a profound awareness that becomes a guiding light in the process of recovery.

Mindfulness: A Present-Centered Awareness

At its essence, mindfulness involves cultivating a present-centered awareness—a conscious and non-judgmental attention to thoughts, feelings, and sensations as they unfold. In the context of opiate addiction recovery, mindfulness serves as a compass, allowing individuals to navigate the complexities of cravings, emotions, and the underlying causes of their addiction with clarity and self-compassion.

Meditation: Cultivating Inner Stillness

Meditation, a sibling to mindfulness, delves deeper into cultivating inner stillness. Through various meditation techniques, individuals embark on a journey of self-discovery and tranquility. Whether through focused attention on the breath, body scan exercises, or lovingkindness meditation, these practices become powerful tools in dismantling the internal turmoil often associated with addiction.

Breaking the Cycle of Reactivity

The intertwining cycle of reactivity and substance use is a central theme in addiction. Mindfulness disrupts this cycle by introducing a pause—a moment of conscious awareness. By observing cravings and triggers without immediate reaction, individuals reclaim agency over their responses. This shift from reactivity to mindful response is a cornerstone in breaking free from the habitual patterns of addiction.

Embracing Emotional Resilience

Mindfulness and meditation foster emotional resilience—a crucial asset in the recovery journey. By developing an accepting and compassionate stance toward emotions, individuals can navigate the emotional complexities that often underlie addiction. These practices provide a space for individuals to sit with discomfort, explore its roots, and gradually cultivate emotional well-being.

Neuroplasticity and Mind-Body Connection

Scientifically, mindfulness and meditation have been linked to neuroplasticity—the brain's ability to reorganize itself. Regular practice can lead to structural changes in the brain, reinforcing healthier patterns of thought and behavior. The mind-body connection is illuminated, emphasizing that the health of the mind profoundly influences the health of the body—a principle foundational to holistic healing.

Success Stories: Inner Transformation

Anna's journey exemplifies the power of mindfulness and meditation in recovery. Struggling with the aftermath of opiate addiction, she turned to mindfulness to confront her internal struggles. Through consistent practice, Anna experienced an inner transformation. Mindfulness became a compass guiding her through cravings, and meditation provided a sanctuary for self-reflection and healing.

Integration into Holistic Recovery

In holistic healing, mindfulness and meditation seamlessly integrate into comprehensive recovery plans. These practices enhance self-awareness, emotional regulation, and resilience, providing individuals with tools to navigate the complexities of recovery. The chapters ahead will unfold additional facets of holistic healing, each contributing to the rich tapestry of recovery—a tapestry woven with the threads of mindfulness, meditation, and the resilient spirit of those on the path to healing.

Section II
Cultivating Awareness and Managing Cravings: Mindful Techniques

Embarking on the Journey of Self-Discovery

Holistic healing beckons individuals on a journey of self-discovery, providing a toolkit of mindful techniques to cultivate awareness and skillfully manage cravings. As cravings arise, these techniques become beacons of mindfulness—illuminating the path toward understanding, acceptance, and ultimately, transformation.

Mindful Breathing: Anchoring in the Present

Central to managing cravings is the practice of mindful breathing—a simple yet potent technique. By bringing attention to the breath, individuals anchor themselves in the present moment. As the breath becomes a focal point, the swirl of cravings diminishes. This technique empowers individuals to observe cravings without being swept away by them, fostering a sense of steadiness and self-awareness.

Body Scan Meditation: Unraveling Tension

The body scan meditation technique invites individuals to direct their attention to different parts of the body, systematically unraveling tension and promoting awareness. In the face of cravings, this practice becomes a grounding force. By scanning the body, individuals cultivate a heightened awareness of physical sensations, disrupting the intensity of cravings and fostering a sense of detachment.

Urge Surfing: Navigating Cravings Mindfully

Urge surfing is a mindfulness technique specifically tailored to managing cravings. It involves riding the wave of cravings with awareness, observing their rise and fall without judgment. Rather than resisting or succumbing to cravings, individuals become surfers navigating the currents of discomfort. This technique acknowledges cravings as temporary experiences, empowering individuals to respond with patience and resilience.

Mindful Eating: Savoring the Present

Mindful eating extends the principles of mindfulness to the act of consuming food. When applied to cravings, this technique invites individuals to approach the experience with full sensory awareness. By savoring each bite and tuning into the taste, texture, and aroma of food, individuals not only satisfy physical hunger but also cultivate mindfulness, redirecting their attention away from cravings.

Non-Identification: Observing without Attachment

A key aspect of managing cravings mindfully is non-identification. This involves observing cravings without attaching personal significance or judgment. By recognizing cravings as passing phenomena rather than inherent aspects of the self, individuals disentangle their sense of identity from the experience of craving. This shift fosters a greater sense of freedom and self-awareness.

Success Stories: Triumph over Cravings

Alex's journey exemplifies the transformative impact of these mindful techniques. Confronting intense cravings, Alex turned to mindful breathing and urge surfing. By observing cravings without yielding to them, Alex disrupted the habitual patterns of substance use. This success story illuminates the practical application of mindful techniques in navigating and triumphing over cravings.

Holistic Integration into Recovery

As we explore techniques for cultivating awareness and managing cravings, it becomes evident that these practices seamlessly integrate into the holistic fabric of recovery. The chapters ahead will unfold additional dimensions of holistic healing, offering a comprehensive approach that honors the interconnected nature of mind, body, and spirit. Each technique becomes a brushstroke in the canvas of recovery —an artistry of mindfulness, resilience, and the unwavering commitment to self-discovery.

Section III
Yoga and Physical Wellness: Embodied Healing

The Union of Mind and Body

In the realm of holistic healing, yoga emerges as a profound practice— a union of breath, movement, and mindfulness that transcends the boundaries between mind and body. This ancient discipline becomes a cornerstone for individuals seeking recovery, offering a holistic approach to physical wellness and embodied healing.

Yoga Asanas: Moving with Intention

At the heart of yoga are asanas—physical postures that synchronize breath with intentional movement. As individuals engage in these postures, they cultivate a heightened awareness of the body. The deliberate and mindful nature of each movement becomes a metaphor for the intentional choices individuals make in their journey toward recovery.

Breathwork (Pranayama): Cultivating Calm

Pranayama, or breathwork, is a pivotal element of yoga practice. The intentional regulation of breath becomes a tool for cultivating calm and managing stress. For individuals in recovery, breathwork serves as a bridge between the physical and mental realms, providing a means to ground oneself in the present moment and navigate the challenges that may arise.

Mindful Movement: Fostering Presence

Yoga is not merely a series of physical exercises; it is a practice of mindful movement. Through deliberate and conscious engagement with each pose, individuals develop a profound sense of presence. This presence becomes a sanctuary—a space where the mind can retreat from the turbulence of cravings, fostering a tranquil internal environment

Strength and Flexibility: Metaphors for Resilience

The physical benefits of yoga extend beyond flexibility and strength. The postures themselves become metaphors for resilience—bending without breaking, standing firm in the face of challenges. As individuals build physical strength and flexibility, they simultaneously nurture the inner qualities needed for sustained recovery.

Restorative Yoga: Nurturing Self-Care

In the spectrum of yoga practices, restorative yoga takes center stage in nurturing self-care. Emphasizing relaxation and gentle postures, it becomes a balm for individuals healing from the physical and emotional toll of addiction. This practice encourages a gentle turning inward—a vital component of the holistic recovery journey.

Success Stories: Wholeness Rediscovered

Rachel's story exemplifies the transformative power of yoga in recovery. Struggling with the aftermath of addiction, she discovered solace in yoga's mindful movement and breathwork. As she progressed through her practice, Rachel not only regained physical wellness but also unearthed a profound sense of wholeness—rediscovering a connection between mind and body.

Holistic Integration into Recovery

The integration of yoga into the holistic landscape of recovery becomes a testament to the interconnectedness of well-being. The chapters ahead will unfold additional dimensions of holistic healing, each contributing to the harmonious tapestry of recovery—a tapestry woven with the threads of yoga, physical wellness, and the embodied journey toward wholeness.

Section IV
Exercise and Nutrition: Fueling the Recovery Journey

A Holistic Framework for Well-Being

In the expansive terrain of holistic healing, the interplay of exercise and nutrition emerges as a dynamic duo—a holistic framework that nourishes the body, rejuvenates the mind, and fosters resilience in the recovery journey. This symbiotic relationship becomes a cornerstone for individuals seeking a comprehensive approach to well-being.

Exercise: Energizing the Body and Mind

Physical activity, a potent component of holistic healing, extends far beyond the realm of fitness. Exercise becomes a catalyst for releasing endorphins—neurotransmitters that act as natural mood enhancers. Whether through cardiovascular workouts, strength training, or mindful movement practices like yoga, exercise becomes a conduit for individuals to channel their energy positively, reducing stress and enhancing mental clarity.

Building Physical Resilience

The role of exercise in building physical resilience aligns with the overarching goal of recovery. Regular physical activity contributes to improved cardiovascular health, strengthened immune function, and enhanced sleep patterns. As individuals engage in exercise, they embark on a transformative journey—one that extends beyond the immediate benefits of fitness to encompass a comprehensive approach to well-being.

Nutrition: Nourishing the Body and Mind

Nutrition forms the second pillar of this holistic approach. The food individuals consume becomes not only fuel for the body but also a source of essential nutrients that influence mental well-being. A balanced diet rich in vitamins, minerals, and antioxidants contributes to cognitive function, mood regulation, and overall vitality—a crucial foundation for those navigating the complexities of recovery.

Mindful Eating: Conscious Nourishment

Mindful eating, an extension of mindfulness practices, encourages individuals to approach meals with conscious awareness. By savoring each bite, paying attention to hunger and fullness cues, and making intentional choices about food, individuals cultivate a harmonious relationship with nourishment. Mindful eating becomes a bridge between the physical and psychological aspects of recovery.

Hydration: A Cornerstone of Well-Being

Amidst the focus on nutrition, hydration stands as a cornerstone. Optimal hydration supports bodily functions, aids in detoxification, and fosters mental clarity. As individuals prioritize adequate water intake, they lay the groundwork for a holistic approach to well-being—an approach that recognizes the interconnected nature of physical health and mental resilience.

Success Stories: Vitality Regained

John's story exemplifies the transformative impact of exercise and nutrition in recovery. Engaging in regular physical activity not only enhanced his physical well-being but also became a source of empowerment. Coupled with a balanced diet, John regained a sense of vitality, reinforcing the integral role of exercise and nutrition in the holistic recovery journey.

Holistic Integration into Recovery

The chapters ahead will unveil additional layers of holistic healing, each contributing to the intricate mosaic of recovery—a mosaic woven with the threads of exercise, nutrition, and the unwavering commitment to holistic well-being. As individuals embrace the dynamic interplay of these elements, they forge a path toward not only breaking free from addiction but also cultivating a vibrant and resilient life.

5 CHAPTER

PERSONALIZED RECOVERY PLANS

Section I
Assessing Your Situation: A Personal Odyssey

The Crucial First Step

Embarking on the journey of personalized recovery requires a reflective pause—a moment to assess your situation with both honesty and compassion. This pivotal step lays the foundation for crafting a recovery plan tailored to your unique needs, circumstances, and aspirations. The assessment process becomes a personal odyssey—an exploration of the self in the context of addiction and the path to healing.

Self-Reflection: The Mirror Within

Begin by gazing into the mirror within. Self-reflection invites you to explore the intricacies of your relationship with substances, acknowledging the patterns, triggers, and emotions entwined with your journey. This candid self-appraisal, free from judgment, provides valuable insights into the roots of addiction, paving the way for informed decision-making.

Understanding Triggers and Cravings

Delve into the landscape of triggers and cravings—the subtle forces that influence your relationship with substances. Identify environmental cues, emotional triggers, and situational contexts that contribute to cravings. Understanding these dynamics equips you with the awareness needed to navigate challenges and proactively develop strategies for managing triggers.

Assessing Mental and Emotional Well-Being

Your mental and emotional well-being stands as a compass guiding the recovery voyage. Assess the presence of co-occurring mental health issues, such as anxiety or depression, recognizing their impact on addiction. This evaluation provides a holistic understanding of your emotional landscape, informing the integration of therapeutic approaches into your personalized recovery plan.

Exploring Support Systems

Recovery thrives within a supportive ecosystem. Evaluate your existing support systems—relationships, family dynamics, friendships, and community connections. Identify individuals who can serve as anchors in your journey, fostering encouragement, understanding, and non-judgmental support.

Physical Health Assessment

Holistic well-being encompasses physical health. Conduct an assessment of your overall health, taking note of any medical conditions or nutritional imbalances. This examination provides a comprehensive view, allowing for the incorporation of exercise, nutrition, and other physical wellness elements into your personalized recovery plan.

Seeking Professional Guidance

Navigating the assessment process benefits from professional guidance. Seek the support of healthcare professionals, therapists, or addiction specialists. Their expertise facilitates a nuanced understanding of your situation, contributing to the formulation of a recovery plan that aligns with your goals and promotes lasting well-being.

Your Recovery Narrative Unfolds

As you embark on the journey of assessing your situation, recognize that your recovery narrative unfolds uniquely. The chapters ahead will explore the artistry of crafting personalized recovery plans, each stroke contributing to the masterpiece of healing. Your odyssey is both individual and interconnected—an exploration that intertwines the wisdom of self-discovery with the guidance of professionals, friends, and the resilience within.

Creating a Personalized Profile:
Crafting Tailored Recovery Your Recovery Blueprint

Crafting a tailored recovery plan begins with creating a personalized profile—a blueprint that reflects the nuances of your journey, strengths, and aspirations. This process is an invitation to shape a recovery narrative uniquely yours, merging self-discovery with evidence-based strategies to cultivate a sustainable path forward.

Understanding Your Substance Use Patterns

Begin by delineating your substance use patterns. Reflect on the types of substances used, frequency, and quantities consumed. This nuanced understanding forms the cornerstone for developing strategies that address specific aspects of your relationship with substances.

Identifying Motivations for Change

Explore the motivations propelling your desire for change. Whether driven by health concerns, personal growth, or the desire to mend relationships, identifying these motivations anchors your recovery plan in purpose. Motivations become guiding lights, illuminating the path during moments of challenge.

Mapping Triggers and High-Risk Situations

Map out triggers and high-risk situations that fuel cravings. These can range from specific environments to emotional states. By charting these elements, you gain insights into potential pitfalls and lay the groundwork for proactive coping mechanisms to navigate challenging moments.

Considering Co-Occurring Mental Health Factors

A personalized profile acknowledges co-occurring mental health factors. Evaluate any existing mental health conditions and their interplay with substance use. This insight informs the integration of therapeutic approaches that address both addiction and mental well-being.

Strengths and Resilience: Unveiling Your Assets

Every individual possesses unique strengths and resilience. Identify your innate qualities—coping mechanisms, support systems, and personal strengths. Leveraging these assets empowers you to navigate challenges and build a resilient foundation for sustained recovery.

Establishing Realistic Goals

Set realistic and attainable goals aligned with your recovery journey. These goals act as milestones, providing a sense of direction and achievement. Break down larger objectives into manageable steps, fostering a gradual and sustainable progression.

Building a Support Network

A personalized recovery plan is not crafted in isolation. Identify and engage with a support network—friends, family, support groups, or mentors. These connections offer encouragement, understanding, and accountability, contributing to the robustness of your recovery framework.

Regular Evaluation and Adaptation

Your personalized profile is a living document, subject to evolution. Regularly evaluate your progress, adapting strategies based on changing circumstances and insights gained along the way. Flexibility and openness to adjustment become integral to the dynamic nature of recovery.

Your Recovery, Your Narrative

Creating a personalized profile is an empowering act—an assertion of agency in shaping your recovery narrative. The chapters ahead will delve into the art of translating this profile into actionable strategies, each element contributing to the masterpiece of your unique journey toward lasting well-being.

Section II
Crafting Your Recovery Blueprint: Strategies for Lasting Well-Being

Tailoring Strategies to Your Unique Journey

Crafting your recovery blueprint involves translating your personalized profile into actionable strategies—tailored interventions that resonate with your unique journey. This process is an art, blending evidencebased approaches with the intricate brushstrokes of your strengths, motivations, and aspirations.

Holistic Approach: Mind, Body, and Spirit

A holistic recovery blueprint acknowledges the interconnectedness of mind, body, and spirit. Consider incorporating elements that address not only the physical aspects of addiction but also nurture emotional well-being and spiritual growth. This approach recognizes the multifaceted nature of recovery.

Therapeutic Modalities: A Customized Blend

Select therapeutic modalities that align with your needs. Whether Cognitive-Behavioral Therapy (CBT), Dialectical Behavior Therapy (DBT), or mindfulness-based approaches, the key is customization. Tailor these interventions to resonate with your preferences, providing a meaningful framework for self-reflection and growth.

Medication-Assisted Treatment (MAT): Individualized Support

If appropriate, explore Medication-Assisted Treatment (MAT) options. Engage in informed discussions with healthcare professionals to determine if medications like Suboxone, methadone, or naltrexone align with your recovery goals. The individualized nature of MAT ensures a tailored approach to addressing physiological aspects of addiction.

Mindfulness Practices: Cultivating Presence

Infuse mindfulness practices into your daily routine. Whether through meditation, mindful breathing, or yoga, these practices foster present-centered awareness. Mindfulness becomes a powerful tool for managing cravings, navigating stress, and promoting overall mental well-being.

Physical Wellness: Exercise and Nutrition

Prioritize physical wellness through regular exercise and balanced nutrition. Design an exercise routine that suits your preferences and integrates seamlessly into your lifestyle. Similarly, nourish your body with a nutrition plan that supports overall health, aiding in recovery from the inside out.

Support Networks: Building a Community

Cultivate and strengthen your support network. Engage with support groups, therapy, or peer mentorship programs. These connections provide understanding, accountability, and encouragement—a crucial tapestry of support woven into your recovery journey.

Goal Setting: Milestones of Progress

Set realistic and meaningful goals. Break down larger objectives into manageable steps, creating a roadmap for your recovery journey. Celebrate achievements along the way, reinforcing a sense of progress and motivation.

Regular Evaluation and Adaptation

Continuously evaluate and adapt your recovery blueprint. Be attuned to changes in your circumstances, insights gained, and evolving goals. Flexibility and openness to adjustment ensure that your recovery strategies remain responsive to your dynamic journey. Empowerment through Choices Your recovery blueprint is a canvas of empowerment—a collection of choices and strategies reflecting your commitment to well-being. As you navigate the chapters ahead, each element contributes to the rich tapestry of your recovery narrative—a narrative defined by resilience, self-discovery, and the steadfast pursuit of lasting health and happiness.

Section III
Developing Your Individualized Plan: A Step-by-Step Guide

Step 1: Reflect and Assess

Begin with a reflective self-assessment. Explore your substance use patterns, motivations for change, and triggers. This honest appraisal lays the groundwork for a comprehensive understanding of your unique journey.

Step 2: Identify Goals and Motivations

Clarify your goals and motivations. What drives your desire for change? Whether it's health improvement, personal growth, or mending relationships, articulating your motivations becomes the compass guiding your recovery journey.

Step 3: Map Triggers and High-Risk Situations

Map out triggers and high-risk situations. Identify environments, emotions, or stressors that contribute to cravings. This step allows you to proactively plan strategies for navigating challenges and reinforces your ability to respond effectively.

Step 4: Evaluate Mental and Emotional Well-Being

Assess your mental and emotional well-being. Identify any cooccurring mental health factors that influence your addiction. This evaluation guides the integration of therapeutic approaches that address both substance use and mental health.

Step 5: Recognize Strengths and Resilience

Uncover your strengths and resilience. Identify coping mechanisms, support systems, and personal assets. Leveraging these strengths becomes a vital aspect of crafting a plan that acknowledges and builds upon your inherent capabilities.

Step 6: Set Realistic and Attainable Goals

Set realistic and attainable goals. Break down larger objectives into manageable steps, creating a roadmap for your recovery journey. Setting milestones allows you to track progress and fosters a sense of achievement.

Step 7: Explore Therapeutic Modalities

Explore therapeutic modalities that resonate with you. Whether it's Cognitive-Behavioral Therapy (CBT), mindfulness-based practices, or other evidence-based approaches, choose interventions that align with your preferences and support your journey.

Step 8: Consider Medication-Assisted Treatment (MAT)

If applicable, discuss Medication-Assisted Treatment (MAT) options with healthcare professionals. Explore the potential benefits of medications such as Suboxone, methadone, or naltrexone. The decision should align with your recovery goals and individual needs.

Step 9: Integrate Mindfulness Practices

Infuse mindfulness practices into your routine. Whether through meditation, mindful breathing, or yoga, these practices enhance present-centered awareness, providing valuable tools for managing cravings and navigating stress.

Step 10: Prioritize Physical Wellness

Prioritize physical wellness through regular exercise and balanced nutrition. Design an exercise routine that suits your preferences, and adopt a nutrition plan that supports overall health. Physical well-being contributes significantly to the recovery process.

Step 11: Cultivate Support Networks

Cultivate and strengthen your support networks. Engage with support groups, therapy, or peer mentorship programs. Building connections provides understanding, encouragement, and a sense of community—a cornerstone of sustained recovery.

Step 12: Regularly Evaluate and Adapt

Commit to regular evaluation and adaptation. Periodically reassess your progress, goals, and strategies. Be flexible and open to adjustments, ensuring that your recovery plan remains responsive to your evolving needs.

Your Unique Recovery Journey Unfolds

By following this step-by-step guide, you lay the foundation for a personalized recovery plan that aligns with your individual journey. As you navigate the chapters ahead, each element contributes to the richness of your recovery narrative—a narrative woven with resilience, empowerment, and the promise of lasting well-being

CHAPTER 6

PEER SUPPORT

The Power of Connection: Navigating Recovery Together

The Essence of Peer Support Peer support stands as a beacon in the landscape of recovery—a potent force fueled by the understanding that the journey is often best navigated with companions who share similar paths. At its essence, peer support transcends traditional roles, forming a collective of individuals linked by the common thread of overcoming addiction.

Shared Understanding and Empathy

In the realm of peer support, the power lies in shared understanding. Peers, having weathered similar storms, offer a unique form of empathy born from lived experiences. This shared connection becomes a lifeline—a source of validation, encouragement, and the reassurance that recovery is not a solitary endeavor.

Breaking the Stigma Through Shared Stories

Peer support becomes a vehicle for breaking the chains of stigma surrounding addiction. Through shared stories and open dialogue, individuals reclaim their narratives, dispelling misconceptions and fostering an environment where vulnerability is met with understanding. This collective narrative challenges societal biases, contributing to a culture of empathy and acceptance.

Strength in Diversity

Peer support celebrates the diversity of recovery journeys. In a group of peers, one finds individuals at various stages of recovery, each with a unique perspective. This diversity enriches the collective experience, providing a tapestry of insights, coping strategies, and triumphs that resonate with the multifaceted nature of addiction and recovery.

Building Trust and Accountability

Trust is a cornerstone of peer support. The shared vulnerabilities within a peer group cultivate an atmosphere of trust and non-judgment. In this supportive environment, individuals feel empowered to be authentic, fostering a deep sense of accountability and responsibility to oneself and the group.

Mutual Inspiration and Motivation

Peer support operates as a reciprocal exchange of inspiration and motivation. Witnessing the achievements of peers—small or monumental—becomes a catalyst for personal growth. The collective momentum generated within a supportive community propels individuals forward, reinforcing the belief that recovery is not only possible but also achievable.

Navigating Challenges Together

Recovery is a journey with its share of challenges. Peer support provides a safety net during difficult times. Whether facing triggers, cravings, or setbacks, the group becomes a haven where individuals can share struggles openly, receive guidance, and draw strength from the collective resilience of their peers.

Online and In-Person Communities

In the digital age, peer support extends beyond physical boundaries. Online communities offer accessibility and anonymity, allowing individuals to connect with peers globally. In-person support groups, on the other hand, provide the intimacy of face-to-face connection. The choice between these formats allows for flexibility based on individual preferences and needs.

The Journey Continues

As we explore the dynamics of peer support in the chapters ahead, it becomes evident that the power of connection extends beyond a mere support system. It transforms into a dynamic force—a catalyst for growth, healing, and the collective triumph over addiction. The journey unfolds not only as an individual endeavor but as a shared odyssey where each participant contributes to the collective narrative of recovery.

Section II
Building a Supportive Network: The Pillars of Peer Connection

Creating Your Peer Support Ecosystem

Building a supportive network within the realm of peer connection involves intentional steps to cultivate a community that uplifts, understands, and propels each member toward lasting recovery. These pillars form the foundation of a robust peer support ecosystem.

1. Seek Authentic Connections

Authenticity is the cornerstone of a supportive network. Foster connections where individuals feel safe to share their unfiltered experiences, vulnerabilities, and triumphs. Authenticity breeds trust and solidarity, laying the groundwork for genuine support.

2. Engage in Open Dialogue

Encourage open dialogue within the peer group. Establish a space where individuals can express thoughts, concerns, and insights freely. Open dialogue dismantles barriers, fostering an environment where diverse perspectives contribute to a collective reservoir of knowledge and support.

3. Foster a Culture of Empathy

Empathy forms the lifeblood of peer support. Cultivate a culture where empathy is woven into the fabric of interactions. When individuals feel heard, understood, and cared for, the collective strength of the group deepens, fortifying each member on their journey.

4. Establish Mutual Accountability

Mutual accountability is a key element in a supportive network. Each member plays a role in holding themselves and others accountable for their recovery goals. This shared responsibility strengthens commitment and reinforces the idea that every individual's success contributes to the collective well-being of the group.

5. Embrace Diversity

Celebrate the diversity within the peer community. Recognize that every recovery journey is unique, and each member brings a wealth of experiences. Embracing diversity fosters an inclusive environment where individuals learn from one another, broaden their perspectives, and find inspiration in varied paths to recovery.

6. Provide Encouragement and Validation

Offer encouragement and validation generously. Celebrate milestones, no matter how small, and acknowledge the resilience of each member. Providing positive reinforcement creates a culture of affirmation, boosting confidence and motivation within the peer group.

7. Create Opportunities for Shared Activities

Shared activities bring a sense of camaraderie. Whether in-person or online, creating opportunities for group activities fosters a sense of community. Shared experiences, such as group outings, virtual events, or collaborative projects, strengthen the bonds between peers.

8. Utilize Technology

Mindfully In the digital era, leverage technology mindfully to connect with peers. Online platforms, forums, and support groups provide accessibility and facilitate global connections. However, it's essential to balance virtual interactions with in-person connections to create a comprehensive and well-rounded peer support experience.

9. Establish Clear Boundaries

Clear boundaries are crucial in maintaining a healthy peer support network. Encourage members to communicate openly about personal boundaries and respect the autonomy of each individual. Establishing clear boundaries ensures a safe and secure space for everyone.

10. Encourage Ongoing Learning and Growth

A supportive network is a dynamic ecosystem that evolves with its members. Encourage ongoing learning and personal growth within the group. Sharing resources, insights, and experiences keeps the peer community vibrant, adaptable, and continuously supportive. As you embark on the journey of building your peer support network, remember that each connection forged is a contribution to the collective strength of the group. The upcoming chapters will delve deeper into the dynamics of peer support, exploring how these foundational pillars contribute to sustained recovery and transformative connections.

Section III
Success Stories: Illuminating the Path of Peer Connection

Realizing Triumph Through Shared Narratives

Success stories within the realm of peer support serve as guiding stars, illuminating the path of recovery with the brilliance of lived experiences. These narratives transcend individual journeys, becoming beacons of hope, resilience, and the tangible proof that the power of peer connection can catalyze transformative change.

Rachel's Journey: From Isolation to Community

Rachel's story epitomizes the transformative impact of peer support. Struggling with the isolation that often accompanies addiction, she found solace in a peer group where authenticity and understanding thrived. Through shared experiences, Rachel discovered the strength to confront her challenges, ultimately achieving sustained recovery.

John's Triumph: Overcoming Setbacks with Peer Encouragement

John's journey exemplifies the resilience cultivated within a supportive network. Faced with setbacks, John found strength in the encouragement of his peers. Their unwavering support became the catalyst for his renewed determination, propelling him beyond obstacles toward a resilient recovery.

Maria's Empowerment: Harnessing Collective Wisdom

Maria's experience showcases the power of collective wisdom within a peer community. By actively engaging in open dialogue and embracing diverse perspectives, Maria harnessed the insights of her peers to inform her recovery strategies. This collaborative approach became a cornerstone in her journey toward sustained well-being.

Michael's Redemption: Finding Redemption through Mutual Accountability

Michael's redemption story highlights the significance of mutual accountability. Embracing the collective responsibility within his peer group, Michael found the strength to confront his challenges head-on. The shared commitment to growth and recovery propelled him toward lasting transformation.

Emma's Resilience: Navigating Cravings with Peer Understanding

Emma's story illustrates the resilience cultivated through empathetic peer connections. During moments of intense cravings, Emma found solace in a peer group that understood the complexities of addiction. Their shared experiences provided a lifeline, allowing her to navigate challenges with newfound strength.

David's Renewal: Embracing Diversity in Recovery

David's renewal unfolds as a testament to embracing diversity within a peer support community. Encountering varied paths to recovery within his group, David broadened his perspectives and discovered inspiration in the unique journeys of his peers. This celebration of diversity became a catalyst for his own growth and renewal.

Every Story, a Testament to Peer Power

These success stories weave a tapestry of peer power—a force that transcends individual narratives to create a collective narrative of triumph over addiction. Each story, a testament to the transformative potential of shared understanding, mutual support, and the indomitable spirit cultivated within a thriving peer community.

Your Story, Your Triumph

As you engage in the chapters ahead, remember that your story contributes to the rich tapestry of peer-supported triumphs. The power of connection is not merely a concept; it is a dynamic force that unfolds through the narratives of individuals who, like you, have discovered the strength to triumph over addiction through the collective support of their peers.

Section IV
Real-Life Accounts: Overcoming Addiction Through Peer Support

Stories of Triumph, Resilience, and Shared Victory

Real-life accounts of overcoming addiction through peer support bring to light the transformative impact of shared journeys. These narratives unfold as testaments to the strength cultivated within the bonds of peer connection—stories of triumph, resilience, and the shared victory over the complexities of addiction.

Sam's Journey: Strength in Unity

Sam's journey resonates with the strength found in unity. Struggling with the isolation of addiction, he discovered a peer group that became a second family. United in their pursuit of recovery, Sam and his peers provided unwavering support, proving that the collective strength of a supportive community can overcome even the deepest challenges.

Ava's Empowerment: Rising Above Stigma

Ava's story is one of empowerment rising above stigma. Facing societal judgment, she found solace in a peer community that understood the weight of external perceptions. Together, they dismantled the shackles of stigma, fostering an environment where individuals could embrace their journeys without judgment.

Carlos's Redemption: From Despair to Hope

Carlos's redemption unfolds as a narrative of hope emerging from despair. Through the encouragement of his peers, Carlos confronted the despair of addiction, transforming it into a beacon of hope. The shared victories within his support group propelled him towards a renewed sense of purpose and a life free from substances.

Grace's Renewal: Embracing Vulnerability

Grace's story is a testament to the transformative power of embracing vulnerability. Initially hesitant to share her struggles, Grace found courage within a peer group that valued openness. Through shared vulnerabilities, she discovered a reservoir of strength, ultimately leading to her renewal and sustained recovery.

Tyler's Resilience: Navigating Relapse with Peer Support

Tyler's journey exemplifies resilience in the face of relapse. Instead of judgment, he found understanding and guidance within his peer community. The shared experiences of overcoming setbacks became a source of inspiration, enabling Tyler to navigate the complexities of recovery with renewed determination.

Sophia's Liberation: Breaking the Chains of Isolation

Sophia's liberation is a narrative of breaking free from the chains of isolation. Entrenched in loneliness, she discovered a sense of belonging within her peer group. The shared understanding and camaraderie liberated Sophia from the isolating grip of addiction, fostering a newfound sense of connection.

Each Journey, a Beacon of Hope

These real-life accounts stand as beacons of hope, lighting the way for those navigating the challenges of addiction. Each journey reflects the transformative influence of peer support—its ability to offer understanding, encouragement, and shared triumphs. As you explore these stories, remember that within the pages of peer-supported narratives, you may find echoes of your own journey toward recover

7 CHAPTER

FAMILY INVOLVEMENT

Section I
Rebuilding Relationships: A Crucial Dimension of Recovery

The Role of Family in the Recovery Landscape

Rebuilding relationships stands as a pivotal dimension of the recovery journey, with family involvement playing a crucial role in this transformative process. As individuals navigate the path to recovery, the mending and strengthening of familial bonds become not only a personal endeavor but also a cornerstone for sustained well-being.

1. Understanding the Impact of Addiction on Families

To rebuild relationships, it's essential to first understand the profound impact of addiction on families. The ripple effects extend beyond the individual struggling with substances, affecting the emotional, psychological, and sometimes financial well-being of family members. Acknowledging this impact becomes a foundation for empathetic and constructive communication.

2. Open Dialogue and Honest Communication

The journey of rebuilding relationships commences with open dialogue and honest communication. Family members and individuals in recovery can engage in frank discussions about the challenges faced, the pain experienced, and the shared commitment to healing. Transparent communication becomes a bridge to understanding and rebuilding trust.

3. Establishing Boundaries and Expectations

Clear boundaries and expectations are integral to the rebuilding process. Establishing healthy boundaries safeguards the well-being of all family members, fostering an environment where trust can gradually be rebuilt. Clarity in expectations ensures that each member understands their role in the recovery journey.

4. Family Education and Support

Education is a powerful tool in rebuilding relationships. Providing family members with information about addiction, recovery processes, and coping strategies equips them with the knowledge needed to offer meaningful support. Family support groups and educational resources become pillars of strength, creating a united front against the challenges of addiction.

5. Participating in Family Therapy

Family therapy emerges as a dynamic avenue for rebuilding relationships. Guided by a professional, family therapy sessions facilitate open communication, address underlying issues, and provide a platform for collective healing. These sessions empower families to navigate the complexities of recovery together.

6. Cultivating Empathy and Compassion

The seeds of rebuilding relationships flourish in the soil of empathy and compassion. Family members, through cultivating understanding and compassion, create an environment where individuals in recovery feel supported, valued, and empowered. Compassion becomes a healing force that transcends past struggles.

7. Celebrating Milestones and Progress

Rebuilding relationships is a journey marked by milestones and progress. Celebrating achievements, both big and small, reinforces positive dynamics within the family. Recognizing and acknowledging the efforts of each member contributes to a supportive atmosphere that nurtures the ongoing recovery process.

The Transformative Power of Family Involvement

As we delve into the chapters ahead, the exploration of family involvement will unfold as a narrative of healing, growth, and the transformative power embedded in mending relationships. The threads of understanding, communication, and shared commitment will weave a tapestry of recovery, illustrating that, indeed, the journey to well being is a collective endeavor that embraces and enriches the bonds of family.

Section II
Strategies for Involving and Supporting Family Members

Empowering Families on the Recovery Journey

Involving and supporting family members in the recovery journey requires intentional strategies aimed at fostering understanding, promoting communication, and creating a supportive environment. These strategies empower families to play an active and positive role in the recovery process.

1. Education as a Foundation

Knowledge becomes a cornerstone for family involvement. Providing educational resources on addiction, its impact, and the recovery process equips family members with the understanding needed to navigate challenges. Workshops, literature, and online resources offer valuable insights, demystifying addiction and fostering empathy.

2. Open Communication Channels

Establishing open communication channels is essential. Encourage family members to express their feelings, concerns, and expectations openly. Regular family meetings or counseling sessions provide structured environments where communication can flourish, strengthening bonds and creating a platform for collective problem solving.

3. Setting Clear Boundaries

Setting clear boundaries is a mutual responsibility. Define healthy boundaries that promote well-being and support recovery. This involves establishing expectations for behavior, communication, and shared responsibilities. Clear boundaries contribute to a sense of stability and security within the family unit.

4. Attending Family Therapy Sessions

Family therapy is a dynamic tool for involving and supporting family members. Professional guidance allows families to explore dynamics, address unresolved issues, and develop strategies for supporting the individual in recovery. These sessions promote understanding and healing, fostering a cohesive family unit.

5. Encouraging Self-Care for Family Members

Supporting family members also involves encouraging self-care. The emotional toll of addiction affects everyone in the family. Promote activities that nurture individual well-being, such as counseling, support groups, or personal hobbies. Recognizing and addressing the impact on family members' mental health is crucial for collective resilience.

6. Involvement in Support Groups

Encourage family members to participate in support groups tailored to their needs. Al-Anon and Nar-Anon are examples of support groups specifically designed for families of individuals struggling with addiction. These groups offer a platform for shared experiences, guidance, and mutual support.

7. Celebrating Progress and Small Wins

Celebrate progress and small wins collectively. Acknowledging positive changes reinforces a culture of encouragement and motivates everyone involved. Recognizing the efforts of the individual in recovery and the supportive actions of family members fosters a positive environment conducive to sustained progress.

8. Ongoing Family Education

Education should be an ongoing process. As the recovery journey unfolds, staying informed about any developments in addiction treatment, recovery strategies, or mental health practices ensures that family members remain well-equipped to provide effective support.

A United Front for Recovery

Involving and supporting family members is not only about aiding the individual in recovery but also fostering a collective journey toward healing. These strategies, when implemented intentionally, transform families into a united front—a source of strength, understanding, and unwavering support on the path to lasting recovery.

Section III
Navigating Challenges Together: Strengthening Bonds in Adversity

Facing Challenges as a Unified Family Unit

Navigating challenges is an inevitable aspect of the recovery journey, and for families involved, it becomes an opportunity to strengthen bonds and foster resilience. As the family unit confronts obstacles together, intentional strategies can guide them toward collective growth and unwavering support.

1. Embracing Open Dialogue During Difficult Times

Difficult times call for open dialogue. Encourage family members to express their feelings, concerns, and frustrations in a safe and non judgmental space. Creating an atmosphere where everyone's voice is heard fosters understanding and unity during challenging moments.

2. Reinforcing Clear Communication

Reinforce clear and effective communication. Misunderstandings can arise during times of stress, making transparent communication crucial. Encourage family members to communicate their needs and expectations clearly, minimizing the potential for misinterpretation and promoting a shared understanding of the challenges at hand.

3. Utilizing Family Support Networks

Tap into family support networks during challenging times. Whether through extended family, friends, or community resources, these networks can provide additional layers of support. Strengthening connections outside the immediate family unit widens the circle of understanding and assistance.

4. Seeking Professional Guidance

When challenges seem overwhelming, seeking professional guidance is a proactive step. Family counseling or therapy sessions offer a structured environment where challenges can be addressed with the guidance of a trained professional. These interventions provide strategies for coping, resolving conflicts, and fostering a healthier family dynamic.

5. Emphasizing Individual and Collective Self-Care

Emphasize the importance of self-care for both individuals in recovery and family members. Navigating challenges can be emotionally taxing, and prioritizing self-care activities ensures that each family member is equipped to contribute positively to the collective well-being.

6. Acknowledging Progress Amidst Setbacks

During challenging times, it's crucial to acknowledge progress amidst setbacks. Celebrate the small victories and individual efforts that contribute to the overall recovery journey. Recognizing achievements, no matter how incremental, reinforces a positive outlook and motivates everyone involved to persevere.

7. Cultivating Resilience as a Family Unit

Cultivate resilience as a family unit. Acknowledge that setbacks are part of the recovery process, and facing them together builds collective strength.

Embracing resilience means learning and growing from challenges, reinforcing the family's ability to overcome adversity and emerge stronger.

8. Reflecting and Learning from Challenges

Use challenges as opportunities for reflection and learning. Engage in open discussions about what worked, what didn't, and how the family can collectively adapt and grow. Each challenge becomes a stepping stone for continuous improvement and strengthened familial bonds.

A Unified Front in the Face of Challenges

As families navigate challenges together, the experience becomes a testament to their resilience, commitment, and capacity for growth. By employing these strategies, families can emerge from difficult times not only stronger but also more united—a formidable and unwavering front in the pursuit of sustained recovery and well-being.

Section IV
Addressing Common Family Dynamics in the Recovery Process

Navigating Familial Dynamics on the Road to Recovery

Understanding and addressing common family dynamics is paramount in creating a supportive environment for the recovery process. As families embark on this journey together, acknowledging and addressing these dynamics becomes a catalyst for healing, growth, and sustained well-being.

1. Enabling Behaviors and Boundaries

Enabling behaviors, often rooted in a desire to protect, can inadvertently impede the recovery process. Addressing this dynamic involves establishing clear boundaries. Family members must learn to differentiate between support and enabling, fostering an environment that encourages responsibility and personal accountability.

2. Codependency and Independence

Codependency, a common challenge in familial dynamics, can hinder individual and collective growth. Shifting towards interdependence rather than codependence involves fostering independence within each family member. Encourage autonomy, self-discovery, and a healthy balance between supporting one another and fostering individual well-being.

3. Communication Patterns and Misunderstandings

Family communication patterns play a significant role in the recovery process. Addressing miscommunication involves fostering open dialogue. Recognize and challenge unhealthy communication habits, encouraging family members to express themselves honestly and actively listen to one another.

4. Stigma and Judgment

Stigma and judgment can strain familial relationships. Addressing this dynamic requires education and empathy. Provide family members with resources to understand addiction better, dispel myths, and challenge stigmatizing beliefs. Encourage open discussions to replace judgment with compassion and support.

5. Role Transitions and Expectations

Recovery often involves role transitions within the family. Addressing changing expectations requires flexibility. Families must adapt to new roles, allowing individuals in recovery the space to redefine themselves while ensuring that everyone's needs and responsibilities are communicated and respected.

6. Resentment and Forgiveness

Resentment can linger from past experiences, hindering progress. Addressing this dynamic involves cultivating forgiveness. Encourage family members to express their feelings, acknowledge the impact of addiction on relationships, and work towards forgiveness as a collective process that facilitates healing and renewal.

7. Emotional Expression and Support

Differences in emotional expression can impact family dynamics. Addressing this involves validating diverse emotional responses. Recognize that family members may express emotions differently and emphasize the importance of supporting one another without judgment, fostering an emotionally safe environment.

8. Cultivating a Culture of Empathy

Cultivating a culture of empathy is foundational. Addressing family dynamics involves developing empathy for each member's journey. Encourage active listening, perspective-taking, and a genuine understanding of the challenges faced by both the individual in recovery and family members.

A Collective Journey of Healing

Addressing common family dynamics is an ongoing process that aligns with the evolving nature of recovery. As families engage in open communication, set healthy boundaries, and foster understanding, they contribute to a collective journey of healing—one that transcends challenges, cultivates resilience, and paves the way for lasting recovery and strengthened familial bonds.

8 CHAPTER

LIFESTYLE CHANGES

Section I
Breaking Habits: Transforming Daily Routines for Lasting Recovery

The Significance of Lifestyle Changes in Recovery

Breaking habits is a fundamental aspect of the recovery journey, as it involves transforming daily routines and cultivating a lifestyle conducive to sustained well-being. Lifestyle changes serve as a catalyst for breaking free from the grip of addiction and establishing a foundation for lasting recovery.

1. Understanding Habit Loops and Triggers

Breaking habits requires an understanding of habit loops and triggers. Identify the cues that prompt addictive behaviors and the subsequent routines. By recognizing these patterns, individuals can interrupt the habit loop, replacing destructive routines with healthier alternatives.

2. Creating a Structured Daily Routine

Establishing a structured daily routine is instrumental in breaking free from old habits. A predictable schedule helps create stability, reducing the likelihood of impulsivity or succumbing to triggers. Structure provides a framework for incorporating positive habits and minimizing opportunities for relapse.

3. Introducing Healthy Rituals

Replacing addictive habits with healthy rituals is a transformative step. Introduce activities that promote well-being, such as morning meditation, exercise, or creative pursuits. Healthy rituals not only fill the void left by old habits but also contribute to a positive and fulfilling lifestyle.

4. Identifying and Managing Triggers

Identification and management of triggers are crucial components of breaking habits. Recognize situations, emotions, or environments that trigger cravings and develop strategies to navigate them effectively. This may involve avoiding certain situations initially and gradually building resilience through exposure.

5. Establishing Supportive Social Circles

Social circles play a pivotal role in habit-breaking. Surrounding oneself with supportive and understanding individuals enhances the likelihood of success. Communicate openly with friends and family about the desire for positive change, fostering an environment that encourages growth and recovery.

6. Mindful Decision-Making

Mindful decision-making is key to breaking habits. Encourage individuals to pause, reflect, and make intentional choices aligned with their recovery goals. Mindfulness practices, such as deep breathing or mindfulness meditation, enhance self-awareness and empower individuals to make conscious decisions.

7. Engaging in Holistic Health Practices

Holistic health practices contribute significantly to breaking habits. Emphasize the importance of physical, mental, and emotional well-being. Regular exercise, balanced nutrition, and mental health practices like therapy or mindfulness contribute to overall health, reinforcing the foundation for recovery.

8. Celebrating Milestones and Progress

Celebrate milestones and progress throughout the habit-breaking journey. Acknowledge achievements, no matter how small, as they signify positive changes. Celebrations serve as motivation and reinforce the commitment to the ongoing process of breaking habits and embracing a healthier lifestyle.

A Lifestyle of Recovery and Renewal

Breaking habits is not a solitary act but a transformative shift towards a lifestyle of recovery and renewal. By understanding habit dynamics, establishing supportive routines, and embracing positive rituals, individuals can navigate the challenges of breaking free from addiction, paving the way for a fulfilling and sustainable life in recovery.

Section II
Strategies for Adopting a Healthier Lifestyle

Building Foundations for Lasting Well-being

Adopting a healthier lifestyle is a pivotal step in the recovery journey, setting the stage for sustained well-being. These strategies empower individuals to cultivate habits, routines, and practices that align with their recovery goals, fostering a positive and transformative lifestyle.

1. Mindful Nutrition and Hydration

Mindful nutrition forms the cornerstone of a healthier lifestyle. Encourage balanced and nourishing meals, emphasizing the role of proper hydration. Educate individuals on the impact of nutrition on physical and mental well-being, empowering them to make informed choices that support their recovery.

2. Regular Exercise and Physical Activity

Regular exercise contributes to both physical and mental health. Advocate for incorporating exercise into daily routines, whether through structured workouts, outdoor activities, or recreational sports. Physical activity not only promotes fitness but also serves as a natural outlet for stress and tension.

3. Quality Sleep Hygiene

Quality sleep is paramount for overall well-being. Emphasize the importance of sleep hygiene— establishing consistent sleep patterns, creating a conducive sleep environment, and avoiding stimulants before bedtime. Quality sleep enhances mood, cognitive function, and supports the body's natural healing processes.

4. Mindfulness and Stress Reduction Techniques

Incorporate mindfulness and stress reduction techniques into daily life. Practices such as meditation, deep breathing exercises, or yoga contribute to emotional balance and resilience. These techniques empower individuals to manage stressors effectively, reducing the risk of turning to harmful coping mechanisms.

5. Cultivating Hobbies and Interests

Cultivating hobbies and interests provides a constructive outlet for creativity and enjoyment. Encourage individuals to explore activities that align with their passions, fostering a sense of purpose and fulfillment. Hobbies serve as positive alternatives to addictive behaviors, contributing to a healthier lifestyle.

6. Building Supportive Social Connections

Building supportive social connections is integral to a healthier lifestyle. Foster relationships with individuals who share similar values and goals. Supportive social circles provide encouragement, understanding, and a sense of belonging, reinforcing the foundation for lasting recovery.

7. Continued Learning and Personal Growth

Stimulate continued learning and personal growth. Engaging in educational pursuits, skill development, or pursuing personal goals contributes to a sense of achievement and purpose. The pursuit of knowledge and growth reinforces a positive mindset and commitment to ongoing improvement.

8. Establishing Healthy Boundaries

Establishing healthy boundaries is vital for maintaining a healthier lifestyle. Encourage individuals to set limits on activities, relationships, and commitments that may compromise their well-being. Healthy boundaries safeguard personal space and reinforce the principles of self-care. Embracing a Lifestyle of Recovery These strategies form a holistic approach to adopting a healthier lifestyle, creating a framework for sustained recovery and well-being. By integrating mindful practices, nourishing routines, and positive connections, individuals embark on a transformative journey—a lifestyle of recovery that goes beyond breaking habits to embrace a renewed, fulfilling, and resilient way of living.

Section III
Lifestyle Changes Strategies for Adopting a Healthier Lifestyle

Empowering Change through Practical Approaches

Adopting a healthier lifestyle is a transformative journey that involves practical strategies aimed at fostering positive habits and overall well-being. These actionable approaches empower individuals to navigate the path of recovery with intentionality and resilience.

1. Setting Clear, Achievable Goals

Initiate the journey toward a healthier lifestyle by setting clear and achievable goals. Break down overarching objectives into manageable steps. These smaller, attainable milestones not only provide a sense of accomplishment but also pave the way for sustained progress and motivation.

2. Creating a Supportive Environment

Crafting a supportive environment is instrumental in adopting a healthier lifestyle. Surround oneself with individuals who encourage positive choices and share similar wellness goals. A supportive network fosters accountability, understanding, and collective motivation on the journey to recovery.

3. Establishing a Consistent Routine

Consistency is key in lifestyle changes. Establish a daily routine that incorporates healthy habits such as regular meals, exercise, and adequate sleep. A structured routine provides stability, reduces uncertainty, and creates a foundation for sustainable lifestyle modifications.

4. Mindful Decision-Making

Embrace mindful decision-making as a guiding principle. Encourage individuals to pause, reflect, and make conscious choices aligned with their well-being. Mindfulness enhances self-awareness, allowing individuals to navigate situations, triggers, and temptations with greater clarity and intention. 5. Learning and Practicing Stress Management Stress management is integral to a healthier lifestyle. Teach and practice stress-reducing techniques such as deep breathing, meditation, or progressive muscle relaxation. These tools equip individuals to cope with stressors effectively, minimizing the likelihood of resorting to unhealthy coping mechanisms.

6. Fostering a Positive Mindset

Cultivate a positive mindset to navigate the challenges of lifestyle changes. Encourage individuals to focus on progress, celebrate achievements, and learn from setbacks. A positive outlook serves as a powerful motivator, reinforcing the belief in one's ability to create lasting change.

7. Exploring New Activities and Interests

Embrace novelty by exploring new activities and interests. Engaging in diverse pursuits not only adds richness to life but also provides alternatives to previous habits. The exploration of interests contributes to personal growth, creating a dynamic and fulfilling lifestyle.

8. Reflecting and Adjusting Along the Journey

Emphasize the importance of reflection and adjustment on the journey to a healthier lifestyle. Periodically review goals, assess progress, and adapt strategies as needed. This dynamic approach allows individuals to tailor their path, accommodating changes in circumstances and personal growth. A Journey of Empowerment and Renewal By implementing these practical strategies, individuals embark on a journey of empowerment and renewal. Each step contributes to the creation of a healthier lifestyle—one grounded in intentional choices, supported by a positive environment, and fueled by the resilience to navigate challenges. This transformative process extends beyond recovery, fostering a life characterized by vitality, purpose, and sustained well-being.

Section IV
Hobbies and Passion Projects: Igniting Joy in the Journey

Rediscovering Purpose through Personal Pursuits

In the pursuit of a healthier lifestyle, incorporating hobbies and passion projects becomes a transformative strategy. These endeavors not only provide avenues for creativity and joy but also play a crucial role in redirecting focus, fostering fulfillment, and promoting sustained well-being.

1. Identifying Personal Interests

Begin by identifying personal interests and passions. Encourage individuals to reflect on activities that bring them joy, whether long-loved hobbies or undiscovered interests. This introspective process lays the foundation for choosing pursuits that align with their unique preferences and inclinations.

2. Creating a Personalized Hobby List

Crafting a personalized hobby list involves compiling a range of potential activities. From artistic pursuits like painting or writing to physical activities like hiking or dancing, the list should reflect a diverse array of interests. This ensures that individuals have options that resonate with different aspects of their well-being.

3. Starting Small and Building Consistency

Embarking on hobbies doesn't necessitate grand gestures. Encourage individuals to start small, dedicating manageable amounts of time to their chosen pursuits. Consistency is key—frequent, shorter sessions can be more effective than sporadic, lengthy ones, promoting the integration of hobbies into daily life.

4. Exploring New Horizons

Encourage exploration of new horizons by trying activities beyond one's comfort zone. The discovery of novel interests contributes to personal growth and expands the scope of potential hobbies. This willingness to explore fosters adaptability and enriches the journey of lifestyle changes.

5. Collaborative Projects and Group Activities
Engaging in collaborative projects or group activities adds a social dimension to hobbies. This fosters connections with like-minded individuals, providing a supportive community. Whether through art classes, book clubs, or sports leagues, shared hobbies contribute to a sense of belonging and mutual encouragement.

6. Balancing Relaxation and Challenge

Optimal enjoyment is found in balancing relaxation and challenge within hobbies. Activities should offer a mix of comfort and stimulation, allowing individuals to unwind while also experiencing a sense of accomplishment. This equilibrium contributes to a positive and sustainable engagement with hobbies.

7. Tracking Progress and Celebrating Achievements

Encourage the tracking of progress and the celebration of achievements within hobbies. Whether mastering a new skill or completing a project, recognizing personal growth fosters a sense of pride and motivation. Celebrations become markers of success on the journey to a healthier and more fulfilling lifestyle.

8. Adapting Hobbies to Evolving Interests

As individuals evolve, so may their interests. Emphasize the flexibility to adapt hobbies to changing preferences and circumstances. This dynamic approach ensures that hobbies remain a source of joy and enrichment throughout different phases of the recovery journey.

A Tapestry of Joy and Purpose

By weaving hobbies and passion projects into the fabric of a healthier lifestyle, individuals craft a tapestry of joy and purpose. These pursuits not only enhance overall well-being but also contribute to a life characterized by fulfillment, creativity, and a renewed sense of identity. In the realm of lifestyle changes, hobbies emerge as vibrant threads that intricately connect individuals to a more vibrant and meaningful existence.

Section V
Rediscovering Joy and Purpose in Life

A Transformation Beyond Recovery

Rediscovering joy and purpose in life is a profound aspect of the transformative journey toward a healthier lifestyle. It transcends recovery, delving into the essence of well-being and the cultivation of a life imbued with meaning, passion, and sustained fulfillment.

1. Aligning with Personal Values

The quest for joy and purpose begins by aligning with personal values. Encourage individuals to reflect on what truly matters to them. This introspective process establishes a foundation for making choices and pursuing activities that resonate with their core beliefs and aspirations.

2. Connecting with Meaningful Relationships

Meaningful relationships play a pivotal role in rediscovering joy. Foster connections with individuals who contribute positively to one's life. Whether with family, friends, or supportive communities, these relationships become anchors, providing a sense of belonging and shared joy.

3. Engaging in Acts of Kindness and Contribution

Acts of kindness and contribution amplify joy and purpose. Encourage individuals to engage in altruistic activities, whether small gestures or more significant contributions to their communities. The act of giving back not only benefits others but also fosters a profound sense of fulfillment and purpose.

4. Cultivating a Positive Mindset

Cultivating a positive mindset is fundamental. Guide individuals to focus on gratitude, celebrate achievements, and embrace an optimistic outlook. A positive mindset acts as a powerful lens, allowing individuals to perceive life's challenges as opportunities for growth and sources of resilience.

5. Embracing Personal Growth and Learning

Embrace personal growth as a lifelong journey. Encourage continuous learning, skill development, and the pursuit of personal goals. The commitment to growth fosters a sense of achievement and progress, contributing to an enriched and purposeful life.

6. Mindful Living and Presence

Mindful living involves being present in each moment. Guide individuals to savor the richness of their experiences, whether mundane or extraordinary. Practicing mindfulness enhances awareness, allowing for a deeper connection with one's surroundings and the inherent joy present in everyday life.

7. Setting and Achieving Meaningful Goals

Setting and achieving meaningful goals is a dynamic process. Assist individuals in defining realistic and purpose-driven goals. These goals become milestones in the journey, each accomplishment contributing to a sense of purpose, direction, and an overall fulfilling life.

8. Creating a Life Vision

Encourage the creation of a life vision—a personalized roadmap for the future. This involves envisioning the desired state of one's life, considering aspirations, values, and passions. A life vision becomes a guiding light, directing individuals toward a purposeful and joy-filled existence.

A Holistic Tapestry of Well-Being

Rediscovering joy and purpose in life weaves a holistic tapestry of well-being. It goes beyond the absence of addiction, encapsulating a vibrant, purpose-driven, and joyful existence. In the realm of lifestyle changes, this rediscovery becomes the essence of sustained recovery—a life marked by the richness of experiences, meaningful connections, and an unwavering sense of purpose.

9 CHAPTER

FRONTIERS IN ADDICTION SCIENCE

Section I
Cutting-Edge Research: Unveiling Insights into Addiction and Recovery

Navigating the Pinnacle of Scientific Exploration

In the dynamic landscape of addiction science, cutting-edge research propels us toward a deeper understanding of addiction mechanisms, effective interventions, and the complexities of recovery. This exploration at the forefront of scientific inquiry unveils groundbreaking insights that hold the promise of transforming the trajectory of addiction treatment.

1. Neuroscience Advancements

Delve into the forefront of addiction science through the lens of neuroscience advancements. Explore how neuroimaging techniques, such as functional magnetic resonance imaging (fMRI) and positron emission tomography (PET), unravel the intricate neural pathways associated with addiction. These technologies provide unprecedented insights into the brain's response to substances and the potential for neural rewiring in recovery.

2. Genomic Discoveries

Unlock the secrets encoded in our genes through genomic discoveries. Cutting-edge research explores the genetic factors influencing susceptibility to addiction and responses to treatment. Genomic insights pave the way for personalized interventions, tailoring treatment approaches based on an individual's unique genetic makeup.

3. Pharmacological Innovations

Embark on a journey into pharmacological innovations that redefine addiction treatment. Explore novel medications targeting specific receptors and neural circuits implicated in addiction. From opioid receptor modulators to medications addressing cravings and withdrawal symptoms, these advancements offer new avenues for medication-assisted treatment with improved efficacy and reduced side effects.

4. Precision Medicine in Addiction Treatment

Enter the era of precision medicine tailored to the individual. Cutting-edge research explores how genetic, environmental, and lifestyle factors interact to shape addiction vulnerabilities. Precision medicine allows for personalized treatment plans, optimizing interventions for each person's unique profile and increasing the likelihood of successful recovery.

5. Digital Health and Therapeutic Technologies

Navigate the integration of digital health and therapeutic technologies in addiction research. Explore the use of smartphone applications, virtual reality, and wearable devices to monitor and support individuals in recovery. These technological innovations enhance accessibility, engagement, and real-time interventions, revolutionizing the landscape of addiction care.

6. Behavioral Interventions and Cognitive Enhancements

Uncover the latest in behavioral interventions and cognitive enhancements. From cognitive-behavioral therapy (CBT) advancements to innovative therapeutic modalities, explore how research is shaping more effective approaches to addressing the psychological aspects of addiction. Cognitive enhancements offer promising tools to bolster cognitive functions crucial for recovery.

7. Emerging Modalities in Psychotherapy

Peer into emerging modalities in psychotherapy designed to address the multifaceted nature of addiction. From mindfulness-based therapies to experiential modalities, cutting-edge research illuminates the efficacy of these approaches in promoting emotional regulation, self-awareness, and resilience in the recovery process.

8. Understanding the Social Determinants

Unravel the impact of social determinants on addiction and recovery. Cutting-edge research examines how factors such as socioeconomic status, cultural influences, and community support shape addiction vulnerabilities and treatment outcomes. Understanding these determinants informs more comprehensive and culturally sensitive approaches to addiction care.

The Horizon of Hope and Discovery

As we embark on these new frontiers in addiction science, the horizon unfolds with hope and discovery. Cutting-edge research not only enhances our understanding of addiction but also propels us toward innovative, targeted interventions that hold the potential to redefine the landscape of addiction treatment and pave the way for more effective, personalized, and compassionate approaches to recovery.

Section II
Exploring the Latest Breakthroughs in Addiction Science

Unveiling Transformative Discoveries Shaping the Future

Dive into the forefront of addiction science, where groundbreaking research is reshaping our understanding of addiction and revolutionizing treatment paradigms. The latest breakthroughs illuminate new pathways for intervention, offering hope and promise in the quest for effective and compassionate approaches to addiction and recovery.

1. Neuroplasticity and Healing

Explore the realm of neuroplasticity—a frontier that underscores the brain's remarkable capacity for healing and adaptation. Recent breakthroughs reveal how the brain's structure and function can be positively influenced by various interventions, offering renewed optimism for recovery outcomes. Understanding neuroplasticity informs interventions that harness the brain's inherent ability to reorganize and recover.

2. Microbiome Influence on Mental Health

Enter the emerging field of research on the gut-brain axis and its impact on mental health, including addiction. Recent studies delve into the intricate relationship between the microbiome—microorganisms residing in the digestive system—and mental well-being. These findings open new avenues for understanding how gut health influences addiction susceptibility and recovery trajectories.

3. Epigenetics and Addiction Vulnerability

Uncover the role of epigenetics in shaping addiction vulnerability. Recent breakthroughs illuminate how environmental factors can modify gene expression, influencing an individual's predisposition to addiction. Epigenetic insights offer a nuanced understanding of the interplay between genetics and environmental influences, guiding more targeted and personalized approaches to addiction treatment.

4. Precision Psychiatry

Embark on the era of precision psychiatry, where advancements in diagnostic tools and personalized treatment plans are transforming mental health care. Recent breakthroughs in precision psychiatry offer tailored interventions based on an individual's unique biological, genetic, and environmental factors. This approach holds significant promise in optimizing addiction treatment strategies.

5. Neurofeedback and Brain Training

Navigate the realm of neurofeedback and brain training as cutting-edge interventions in addiction science. Recent breakthroughs explore how real-time monitoring of brain activity and targeted training interventions can contribute to addiction recovery. These innovative techniques empower individuals to regulate their brain function, fostering improved emotional resilience and cognitive control.

6. Immersive Virtual Reality Therapy

Immerse into the realm of virtual reality therapy, a transformative breakthrough in addiction treatment. Recent studies demonstrate the efficacy of immersive virtual reality experiences in simulating real-life scenarios for therapeutic purposes. This novel approach provides a safe and controlled environment for individuals to confront and navigate triggers, contributing to desensitization and coping skill development.

7. Neurostimulation Techniques

Delve into neurostimulation techniques as emerging modalities in addiction science. Recent breakthroughs explore the potential of non-invasive brain stimulation, such as transcranial magnetic stimulation (TMS) and transcranial direct current stimulation (tDCS), in modulating neural circuits implicated in addiction. These techniques hold promise as adjuncts to traditional therapies, offering novel avenues for intervention.

8. Blockchain Technology in Addiction Research

Explore the application of blockchain technology in addiction research, a frontier at the intersection of science and data security. Recent breakthroughs leverage blockchain to enhance the transparency, integrity, and accessibility of addiction research data. This innovation ensures a secure and decentralized platform for sharing findings, fostering collaboration, and advancing the collective understanding of addiction.

A Tapestry of Innovation and Hope

As we explore the latest breakthroughs in addiction science, a tapestry of innovation and hope unfolds. These discoveries not only deepen our understanding of addiction but also offer transformative interventions that hold the potential to revolutionize the landscape of addiction care. Through ongoing exploration and integration of these breakthroughs, we glimpse a future where individuals facing addiction can access personalized, effective, and forward-thinking treatments, marking a profound shift in the trajectory of recovery.

Section III
Promising Technologies: Catalysts for Innovation in Addiction Research

Pioneering Solutions at the Intersection of Technology and Recovery

Discover the transformative impact of promising technologies that are reshaping the landscape of addiction research. At the intersection of innovation and recovery, these cutting-edge tools offer novel avenues for understanding, treating, and supporting individuals on their journey toward overcoming addiction.

1. Artificial Intelligence (AI) in Predictive Analytics

Uncover the potential of artificial intelligence (AI) in predictive analytics for addiction research. AI algorithms analyze vast datasets to identify patterns, predict relapse risks, and tailor interventions. This innovative application enhances the precision of treatment plans, adapting strategies in real-time based on individual responses and evolving circumstances.

2. Telehealth and Remote Monitoring

Enter the era of telehealth and remote monitoring as integral components of addiction care. These technologies facilitate access to treatment and support, breaking down barriers of distance and enhancing continuity of care. Remote monitoring tools offer real-time insights, enabling healthcare providers to intervene promptly and adjust treatment plans as needed.

3. Mobile Applications for Recovery Support

Explore the landscape of mobile applications designed to provide ongoing support in addiction recovery. These apps offer a range of features, from mood tracking and coping skill exercises to community forums. Mobile applications empower individuals with tools for self-monitoring, education, and connection, fostering a sense of autonomy and engagement in their recovery journey.

4. Virtual Reality Exposure Therapy (VRET)

Immerse into the realm of Virtual Reality Exposure Therapy (VRET) as a promising technology in addiction treatment. VRET simulates environments related to substance use, allowing individuals to confront and navigate triggers in a controlled setting. This exposure therapy aids in desensitization and the development of effective coping strategies.

5. Blockchain for Secure Data Sharing

Discover how blockchain technology ensures secure data sharing in addiction research. Blockchain's decentralized and tamper-resistant nature enhances the integrity of research data. This innovation promotes transparent collaboration among researchers, safeguards participant privacy, and fosters a collective effort to advance addiction science.

6. Biometric Monitoring Devices

Witness the integration of biometric monitoring devices for personalized health insights. Wearable devices track physiological indicators such as heart rate, sleep patterns, and stress levels. In addiction research, these devices provide objective data for assessing treatment efficacy, understanding triggers, and tailoring interventions based on individual biometrics.

7. Genetic Testing for Personalized Treatment

Explore the application of genetic testing for personalized addiction treatment. Genetic insights inform treatment approaches by identifying genetic markers related to addiction susceptibility and response to medications. This precision medicine approach enables healthcare providers to tailor interventions, maximizing effectiveness and minimizing adverse effects.

8. Machine Learning for Treatment Optimization

Delve into machine learning's role in optimizing addiction treatment. Machine learning algorithms analyze patient data to identify optimal treatment combinations based on individual characteristics. This data-driven approach enhances treatment outcomes by customizing interventions, reflecting the evolving nature of an individual's recovery journey.

Charting a Course for Progress

As these promising technologies continue to chart new territories in addiction research, a course for progress unfolds. The integration of innovative tools enhances our ability to understand addiction complexities, tailor interventions to individual needs, and create a supportive ecosystem for sustained recovery. In this dynamic intersection of technology and recovery, promising technologies stand as catalysts for innovation, offering unprecedented possibilities in the pursuit of effective, accessible, and personalized addiction care.

Section IV
Shaping the Future of Addiction Treatment: The Impact of Technology

A Technological Revolution in the Realm of Recovery

Witness the transformative influence of technology on the future of addiction treatment, ushering in an era of innovation and personalized care. From novel interventions to enhanced support systems, technology is reshaping the landscape of addiction treatment, offering new possibilities for understanding, addressing, and supporting individuals on their journey to recovery.

1. Tailored Interventions through Predictive Analytics

Experience the power of predictive analytics, where technology analyzes vast datasets to anticipate individual needs in addiction treatment. Predictive models identify patterns, predict potential challenges, and adapt interventions in real-time. This tailored approach ensures that treatment strategies align with the unique circumstances and progress of each individual.

2. Remote Access with Telehealth Solutions

Embrace the accessibility and continuity of care facilitated by telehealth solutions. Technology brings treatment and support directly to individuals, overcoming geographical barriers. Telehealth not only enables remote consultations but also integrates virtual therapy sessions, fostering a flexible and patient-centric approach to addiction treatment.

3. On-the-Go Support through Mobile Applications

Engage in on-the-go support with mobile applications designed specifically for addiction recovery. These apps provide a suite of tools, including self-monitoring features, coping mechanisms, and a supportive community. Accessible anytime, anywhere, mobile applications empower individuals with resources to navigate challenges and stay connected to their recovery journey.

4. Immersive Therapy with Virtual Reality (VR)

Immerse in the potential of virtual reality (VR) as a revolutionary tool in addiction therapy. VR exposure therapy allows individuals to confront triggers in a controlled, simulated environment. This immersive experience aids in desensitization, empowering individuals to develop coping skills and face real-world challenges with resilience.

5. Securing Privacy with Blockchain Technology

Experience the heightened security and privacy protection enabled by blockchain technology. In addiction treatment, blockchain ensures the integrity of sensitive data, fostering trust among researchers and participants. This decentralized and tamper-resistant technology establishes a secure foundation for sharing insights and advancing addiction science collaboratively.

6. Objective Monitoring through Biometric Devices

Explore the role of biometric monitoring devices in providing objective insights into an individual's health. Wearable devices track physiological markers, offering real-time data on factors such as stress, sleep, and physical activity. In addiction treatment, this objective monitoring enhances the understanding of triggers and contributes to personalized intervention strategies.

7. Precision Medicine with Genetic Insights

Enter the realm of precision medicine with genetic insights shaping addiction treatment. Genetic testing identifies key markers influencing susceptibility to addiction and response to medications. This personalized approach tailors treatment plans based on an individual's genetic profile, optimizing effectiveness and minimizing adverse effects.

8. Optimized Treatment Paths with Machine Learning

Navigate the landscape of optimized treatment paths through machine learning. Algorithms analyze diverse patient data to identify patterns and recommend personalized interventions. This data-driven approach ensures that treatment plans evolve dynamically, reflecting the changing needs and progress of each individual throughout their recovery journey.

Pioneering a New Era of Recovery

As technology shapes the future of addiction treatment, it pioneers a new era of recovery characterized by personalization, accessibility, and innovation. These advancements not only enhance treatment efficacy but also empower individuals, fostering a collaborative and dynamic approach to overcoming addiction. In this evolving landscape, technology emerges as a catalyst for positive change, offering a beacon of hope for individuals seeking effective, tailored, and supportive paths to recovery.

10 CHAPTER

MOVING FORWARD

Section I
Embracing Change: A Beacon Toward Lasting Recover

Navigating the Journey Beyond Addiction

As we stand at the threshold of Chapter 10, the essence of moving forward lies in embracing change—a dynamic force that propels individuals beyond the grasp of addiction toward a future marked by resilience, growth, and sustained recovery. This chapter serves as a compass, guiding individuals through the transformative journey of change and providing insights into the evolving landscape of addiction recovery.

1. The Inevitability of Change

 Change is an intrinsic part of the human experience, and in the realm of addiction recovery, it becomes a powerful ally. Acknowledge the inevitability of change—whether subtle shifts in mindset, evolving perspectives, or profound transformations. Understanding change as a constant allows individuals to navigate the recovery journey with flexibility and an openness to new possibilities.

2. Cultivating Resilience in the Face of Challenges

Emphasize the role of resilience as individuals confront challenges on the path to recovery. Resilience is the bedrock that enables individuals to bounce back from setbacks, learn from experiences, and persist in their commitment to change. By cultivating resilience, individuals forge a formidable armor against the uncertainties that may arise.

3. Embracing Personal Growth as a Continuous Process

Highlight personal growth as a continuous and evolving process. In recovery, each day presents an opportunity for self-discovery, learning, and advancement. Encourage individuals to embrace the journey of self-improvement, recognizing that growth is not a destination but a perpetual expedition toward a more fulfilling and purposeful life.

4. Forging Connections with Supportive Communities

Explore the significance of forging connections with supportive communities. Whether through peer support groups, online forums, or local networks, communal bonds contribute to a sense of belonging and shared experience. These connections foster a supportive environment where individuals can draw strength, insights, and encouragement from one another.

5. Adapting to Evolving Recovery Modalities

Acknowledge the evolving landscape of recovery modalities, including innovative therapies and technological interventions. Embrace a willingness to explore and adapt to emerging approaches that align with individual needs. This adaptability ensures that recovery strategies remain dynamic and responsive to the diverse and evolving nature of addiction.

6. Celebrating Milestones and Acknowledging Progress

Celebrate milestones along the recovery journey, both big and small. Acknowledge the progress made, recognizing achievements as stepping stones toward lasting recovery. This positive reinforcement reinforces a sense of accomplishment and reinforces the motivation to continue moving forward.

7. Fostering a Future-Oriented Mindset

Encourage a future-oriented mindset that envisions a life beyond addiction. By focusing on aspirations, goals, and the potential for positive change, individuals can shape a vision of their desired future. This forward-looking perspective becomes a driving force, propelling them toward the realization of their dreams.

8. Reflecting on the Journey with Gratitude

Introduce the transformative power of gratitude as individuals reflect on their journey. Expressing gratitude for newfound insights, supportive relationships, and personal growth cultivates a positive outlook. This reflective practice anchors individuals in the present moment, fostering an appreciation for the positive changes that have unfolded.

Guiding the Way to Lasting Recovery

As we embark on Chapter 10, embracing change becomes the guiding principle toward lasting recovery. This chapter serves as a roadmap, navigating individuals through the transformative landscape of recovery, where change is not merely an endpoint but a continuous, empowering process. By embracing change, individuals embark on a journey of self-discovery, resilience, and the unwavering pursuit of a future marked by enduring recovery and well-being.

Section II
Cultivating a Positive Mindset: The Cornerstone of Sustained Recovery

The Transformative Power of Positive Thinking

In the realm of sustained recovery, cultivating a positive mindset emerges as the cornerstone, shaping the trajectory of individuals as they navigate the ongoing journey of change and growth. This section delves into the transformative power of positive thinking, exploring how an optimistic outlook becomes a catalyst for resilience, motivation, and enduring recovery.

1. Recognizing the Impact of Mindset

Acknowledge the profound impact of mindset on the recovery journey. A positive mindset is not merely a fleeting emotion; it becomes a guiding force that influences behaviors, choices, and reactions to challenges. Understanding the significance of mindset empowers individuals to harness its potential in fostering lasting recovery.

2. Shifting Perspectives Toward Possibilities

Encourage individuals to shift their perspectives toward possibilities. A positive mindset reframes challenges as opportunities for growth and change. By viewing setbacks as temporary detours rather than insurmountable obstacles, individuals can approach recovery with a sense of optimism, resilience, and an unwavering belief in their capacity for change.

3. Embracing Self-Compassion and Forgiveness

Highlight the importance of self-compassion and forgiveness within the realm of positive thinking. Recovery is a journey of self-discovery, and acknowledging imperfections and setbacks with compassion fosters a nurturing environment. Embracing forgiveness, both of oneself and others, becomes a powerful catalyst for releasing the burdens of the past and paving the way for positive transformation.

4. Setting Realistic and Motivating Goals

individuals in setting realistic yet motivating goals. A positive mindset thrives on the sense of achievement, and breaking down overarching goals into smaller, manageable steps contributes to a continuous sense of progress. Celebrating these achievements becomes a reinforcing cycle that propels individuals forward in their recovery.

5. Fostering Gratitude Practices

Introduce gratitude practices as a daily ritual in cultivating a positive mindset. Expressing gratitude for the present moment, supportive relationships, and personal milestones anchors individuals in the positive aspects of their journey. Gratitude becomes a guiding force that nurtures an optimistic perspective even in the face of challenges.

6. Surrounding Oneself with Positivity

Encourage the cultivation of a positive environment. Surrounding oneself with positivity, whether through supportive relationships, uplifting activities, or inspirational content, contributes to the maintenance of a constructive mindset. A positive external environment complements and reinforces the internal journey of positive thinking.

7. Affirmations and Positive Self-Talk

Explore the transformative power of affirmations and positive self-talk. Guiding individuals to consciously choose positive language and affirmations shapes their internal dialogue. This intentional shift in self-talk contributes to building self-esteem, resilience, and a belief in one's capacity to overcome challenges.

8. Mindfulness and Present-Moment Awareness

Integrate mindfulness and present-moment awareness into the fabric of positive thinking. Mindfulness practices cultivate an ability to stay present, letting go of past regrets and future anxieties. This heightened awareness allows individuals to approach each moment with clarity, intention, and a positive mindset.

Cultivating Positivity as a Lifelong Practice

As individuals embark on the journey of sustained recovery, cultivating a positive mindset transcends a mere attitude—it becomes a lifelong practice. This section serves as a guide, illuminating the transformative potential of positive thinking in shaping enduring recovery. By fostering a positive mindset, individuals not only navigate the challenges of change but also embrace the boundless possibilities that lie ahead on their path to sustained well-being and fulfillment.

Section III
Beyond Recovery: Crafting a Life of Meaning and Purpose

Transcending the Notion of Recovery

In the final section of Chapter 10, we venture into the realm beyond recovery—a space where individuals not only overcome addiction but also actively craft lives imbued with meaning, purpose, and a profound sense of fulfillment. This transformative journey transcends the conventional notion of recovery, guiding individuals toward a holistic and purpose-driven existence.

1. Reimagining Life Beyond Addiction

Encourage individuals to reimagine life beyond the constraints of addiction. Beyond recovery lies an expansive landscape where personal growth, self-discovery, and the pursuit of one's passions take center stage. By envisioning a life rich in meaning and purpose, individuals embark on a journey that transcends the narrative of overcoming challenges.

2. Identifying Personal Values and Aspirations

Guide individuals in identifying their core values and aspirations. The journey beyond recovery is guided by a compass of personal values that shape decisions and actions. By aligning daily choices with deeply held values, individuals cultivate a sense of authenticity and purpose that serves as a guiding force in their post-recovery lives.

3. Building Meaningful Connections

Emphasize the importance of building meaningful connections in the post-recovery phase. Beyond recovery, the richness of life is often found in genuine relationships and connections with others. Encourage individuals to foster relationships that contribute positively to their well-being, providing a supportive network as they navigate the complexities of life.

4. Exploring Passion Projects and Hobbies

Inspire individuals to explore passion projects and hobbies that bring joy and fulfillment. Beyond the confines of addiction, life opens up to a world of possibilities. Engaging in activities that ignite passion and creativity becomes a source of purpose, contributing to a fulfilling and balanced post-recovery lifestyle.

5. Contributing to the Community

Highlight the transformative impact of contributing to the community. Beyond recovery, individuals discover the profound fulfillment that comes from giving back. Whether through volunteering, mentorship, or community involvement, contributing to the well-being of others becomes a meaningful and purposeful aspect of life.

6. Continuing Personal Growth and Learning

Emphasize the continuation of personal growth and learning. Beyond recovery, life unfolds as an ongoing journey of self-discovery and expansion. Encourage individuals to embrace new challenges, acquire new skills, and pursue opportunities for learning, fostering a mindset of curiosity and continuous development.

7. Cultivating a Mindful and Present Lifestyle

Integrate mindfulness and present-moment awareness into the fabric of post-recovery living. Beyond recovery, a mindful lifestyle allows individuals to savor each moment, appreciate life's nuances, and navigate challenges with resilience. Mindfulness becomes a cornerstone for maintaining balance, gratitude, and a sense of peace.

8. Embracing a Life of Wholeness

Guide individuals to embrace a life of wholeness. Beyond recovery, the integration of physical, mental, and emotional well-being creates a holistic and fulfilling existence. By prioritizing self-care, individuals nurture a sense of wholeness that forms the foundation for a life steeped in meaning, purpose, and enduring contentment.

Crafting a Future of Possibility

As we conclude Chapter 10, the journey beyond recovery unfolds as a canvas of possibility. This section serves as a compass, guiding individuals toward a life rich in meaning, purpose, and fulfillment. By transcending the traditional notion of recovery, individuals embark on a transformative path where every choice, connection, and endeavor contributes to the crafting of a future imbued with infinite possibilities—a life well beyond recovery.

Section IV
Tools and Resources for Building a Fulfilling, Substance-Free Life

Equipping the Journey Beyond with Essential Resources

As individuals transition into the realm beyond recovery, this section provides a toolbox of invaluable tools and resources. These resources empower individuals to navigate the complexities of crafting a fulfilling, substance-free life. From practical strategies to emotional support, each tool serves as a guidepost on the journey toward lasting well-being and fulfillment.

1. Supportive Networks and Peer Communities

Encourage individuals to cultivate supportive networks and engage with peer communities. Connecting with others who share similar experiences fosters a sense of camaraderie and understanding. Peer support groups, both online and in-person, provide a safe space for sharing challenges, victories, and insights, creating a foundation for ongoing encouragement and mutual growth.

2. Professional Counseling and Therapy

the importance of ongoing professional counseling and therapy. Qualified therapists offer tailored guidance, addressing emotional, psychological, and relational aspects of the post-recovery journey. Regular counseling sessions provide individuals with a confidential space to explore personal challenges, set goals, and receive expert support in navigating life's complexities.

3. Continued Education and Skill Development

Emphasize the significance of continued education and skill development. Pursuing learning opportunities and acquiring new skills contribute to personal growth and career advancement. Educational resources, workshops, and vocational training programs empower individuals to build a foundation for a fulfilling and purpose-driven life beyond recovery.

4. Mindfulness and Meditation Practices

Integrate mindfulness and meditation practices into daily life. Mindfulness techniques cultivate present- moment awareness, offering individuals tools to manage stress, enhance focus, and nurture emotional well-being. Whether through guided meditation apps, mindfulness courses, or community-based meditation groups, these practices become anchors for a centered and balanced life.

5. Holistic Wellness Programs

Explore holistic wellness programs that address physical, mental, and emotional well-being. Incorporating activities such as yoga, nutrition counseling, and fitness routines contribute to overall health. Holistic wellness programs provide individuals with a comprehensive approach to self-care, fostering a lifestyle that prioritizes well-rounded health and resilience.

6. Goal-Setting and Planning Tools

Introduce goal-setting and planning tools to assist individuals in crafting a purposeful life. From journaling to specialized goal-setting apps, these tools facilitate the articulation of aspirations and the creation of actionable plans. Setting and tracking goals becomes a tangible and motivating practice that propels individuals toward their envisioned future.

7. Community Outreach and Volunteering Opportunities

Encourage community outreach and involvement in volunteering opportunities. Contributing to the well- being of others fosters a sense of purpose and community connection. Local organizations, charities, and community centers often offer diverse volunteering options, allowing individuals to make a positive impact and build a network of like-minded individuals.

8. Routine Self-Reflection and Journaling

Promote routine self-reflection and journaling as a means of introspection. Journaling provides a reflective space to process thoughts, emotions, and personal insights. This practice supports individuals in gaining clarity, tracking progress, and fostering a deeper understanding of themselves as they navigate the nuances of their substance-free lives.

Empowering the Journey with Resources

As individuals step into the landscape beyond recovery, these tools and resources become empowering allies. This toolbox equips individuals with the practical and emotional support needed to build a fulfilling, substance-free life. By embracing these resources, individuals embark on a journey marked by resilience, purpose, and the ongoing creation of a life imbued with meaning and well-being.

Conclusion: Your Journey, Your Freedom

In concluding this comprehensive guide to overcoming opiate addiction, it's paramount to underscore a fundamental truth: your journey to recovery is uniquely yours, and within it lies the power to reclaim your freedom. The pages of this book have unfolded as a mosaic of insights, methods, and narratives, offering a diverse toolkit to navigate the complex terrain of addiction and chart a course toward lasting well-being.

Embracing change, cultivating a positive mindset, and envisioning a life beyond recovery are not mere concepts—they are living principles that intertwine to form the tapestry of your personal narrative. Your journey is not bound by a predetermined script; rather, it is an evolving story of resilience, growth, and self-discovery.

As you traverse the chapters of your recovery, remember that setbacks do not define you; they are stepping stones in the path toward progress. Each choice, each moment of mindfulness, and each connection forged contributes to the sculpting of a life that transcends the shadows of addiction.

Your freedom is not a destination but a dynamic process—an ongoing journey where you hold the compass. It involves introspection, self-compassion, and the courage to face challenges with unwavering determination. Surround yourself with supportive communities, utilize the resources at your disposal, and celebrate the milestones that mark your progress.

This conclusion serves not as an endpoint but as an invitation—to continue the exploration of your inner landscape, to embrace the transformations that unfold, and to shape a future that resonates with your deepest aspirations. Your journey is a testament to the strength within, a reminder that freedom is not bestowed but reclaimed with every intentional step forward.

As you move beyond the pages of this guide, carry with you the understanding that your journey is a tapestry woven with threads of resilience, hope, and the triumph of the human spirit. May this guide be a companion, a source of inspiration, and a reminder that your freedom is intricately intertwined with the boundless possibilities that await on the horizon of your unique and extraordinary journey.

ABOUT THE AUTHOR

Elijah L. Cooley is a dedicated father, author, and entrepreneur with a passion for making a positive impact through his writing. As someone who has faced personal challenges and triumphs, Elijah brings a unique perspective to his work, blending personal insights with research and practical strategies.

With a commitment to empowering individuals and families affected by addiction, Elijah strives to provide comprehensive resources and support for those on the journey to recovery. Through his writing, he seeks to foster empathy, understanding, and hope in the face of adversity.

Elijah holds a deep appreciation for his readers and the opportunity to share his experiences and knowledge with them. He believes in the transformative power of storytelling and aims to inspire others to embrace change, overcome obstacles, and live fulfilling lives.

When he's not writing, Elijah enjoys spending time with his family, exploring the outdoors, and pursuing his creative passions. He resides in [Location] with his loved ones, where he continues to pursue his mission of making a difference in the world through his writing and advocacy.

Made in the USA
Columbia, SC
31 March 2024

33374431R00048